OSPREY AIRCRAFT OF THE ACES • 29

Bf 109F/G/K Aces of the Western Front 1941-45

11

SERIES EDITOR: TONY HOLMES

OSPREY AIRCRAFT OF THE ACES • 29

Bf 109F/G/K Aces of the Western Front 1941-45

John Weal

OSPREY
AVIATION

Front cover
Eastern front *Experte* (with 202 kills) Major Hermann Graf was appointed to the command of JG(r) 50 in August 1943. This specialist Defence of the Reich unit was tasked with combating US heavy bombers, as well as high-flying RAF reconnaissance aircraft. For this dual role, the *Geschwader* equipped its Bf 109G-6s either with underwing rockets (as depicted here) or additional cannon gondolas (see profile 29). On 6 September Graf claimed two B-17s during the Eighth Air Force's costly, and ineffective, mission against Stuttgart, which was frustrated by increasingly cloudy conditions. The bombers ended up attacking 'targets of opportunity' instead, dropping ordnance over wide tracts of Germany and occupied western Europe – the 100th Bomb Group (BG), for example, dropped its bombs south-west of Paris! In this specially-commissioned artwork by Iain Wyllie, Graf's Bf 109G-6 (Wk-Nr 15913) 'Red 1' is seen just seconds after performing a head-on attack on a formation of B-17Fs from the 92nd BG, which has left one Flying Fortress streaming smoke from its outer port engine. The 92nd lost seven bombers on this day, at least one of which almost certainly fell to Major Graf

Back cover
Basking in Wiesbaden-Erbenheim's autumn sunshine in front of his heavily-dappled 'Red 3' (a Bf 109G-6 of JG 50), Leutnant Gottfried Weiroster enjoys all the comforts of home, courtesy of the 'U.S. AIR CORPS'!

First published in Great Britain in 1999
by Osprey Publishing, Elms Court, Chapel Way, Botley, Oxford, OX2 9LP

ISBN 1 85532 905 0

Edited by Tony Holmes
Page design by TT Designs, T & B Truscott
Cover Artwork by Iain Wyllie
Aircraft Profiles by John Weal
Scale Drawings by Mark Styling
Origination by Grasmere Digital Imaging, Leeds, UK
Printed through Bookbuilders, Hong Kong

00 01 02 03   10 9 8 7 6 5 4 3 2

ACKNOWLEDGEMENTS
The author would like to thank the following individuals for their generous help in providing information and photographs: Paul Groves, Jon Lake, Michael Payne, Dr Alfred Price, Jerry Scutts, Robert Simpson, Tony Wood and *Herren* Holger Nauroth, Willi Reschke and Ernst Wichmann.

BIBLIOGRAPHY

ADERS, GEBHARD and HELD, WERNER, *Jagdgeschwader 51 'Mölders'*. Motorbuch Verlag, Stuttgart, 1985
BARBAS, BERND, *Planes of the Luftwaffe Fighter Aces, vols 1 & 2*. Kookaburra, Melbourne, 1985
BEKKER, CAJUS, *Angriffshöhe 4000: Kriegstagebuch der deutschen Luftwaffe*. Stalling Verlag, Oldenburg, 1964
BENNETT, RALPH, *Ultra in the West: The Normandy Campaign of 1944-45*. Hutchinson, London, 1979
CALDWELL, DONALD, *JG 26: Top Guns of the Luftwaffe*. Orion, New York, 1991
CALDWELL, DONALD, *JG 26: Photographic History of the Luftwaffe's Top Guns*. Airlife, Shrewsbury, 1994
CALDWELL, DONALD, *The JG 26 War Diary: Vol. One 1939-1942*. Grub Street, London, 1996
CALDWELL, DONALD, *The JG 26 War Diary: Vol. Two 1943-1945*. Grub Street, London, 1998

(Bibliography continued on page 96)

For a catalogue of all titles published by Osprey Military, Aviation and Automotive please write to:

Osprey Direct UK, P.O. Box 140, Wellingborough, Northants NN8 4ZA, UK
E-mail: **info@OspreyDirect.co.uk**

Osprey Direct USA, P.O. Box 130, Sterling Heights, MI 48311-0130, USA
E-mail: **info@OspreyDirectUSA.com**

Or visit our website: **http://www.osprey-publishing.co.uk**

CONTENTS

FIRST LINE OF DEFENCE

I t is now generally accepted that the Battle of Britain constituted one of the first major turning points of World War 2. At its close, the hitherto seemingly invincible German Luftwaffe – victorious in Poland, Scandinavia, the Low Countries and France – had, for the first time, failed to achieve its assigned objectives: the neutralisation of the Royal Air Force (RAF), and the subsequent invasion and subjugation of England.

The first *Friedrichs* were delivered to *Stab* JG 51 before the end of the Battle of Britain. The 54 kills marked on the rudder of this rather nondescript machine identify it as one of those flown by Major Werner Mölders. The bottom half of the rudder and the entire engine cowling have been painted yellow

The British have come to regard the Battle as having been 'officially' over, and won, by 31 October 1940. German aviation historians are less arbitrary. They consider the daylight operations (admittedly drastically reduced in scale) flown during the closing weeks of the year, and the attendant night *Blitz*, which continued well into the spring of 1941, as part and parcel of the same campaign. In their view, the ongoing aerial onslaught against Great Britain was only brought to a halt by Hitler's decision to shelve indefinitely his plans for a cross-Channel invasion, and turn his attention instead to other fronts: to the Mediterranean and the Balkans and, ultimately, to the east.

The duration of the Battle may be open to argument, but its effect on the air war in the west was conclusive and irreversible. After a necessary period of rest and recuperation for both sides, the resumption of significant daylight cross-Channel operations early in 1941 set the pattern for the weeks, months and years ahead. Although the Luftwaffe would still be called upon to mount sporadic forays over southern England, its stance in occupied north-western Europe became increasingly defensive as the RAF flexed its new-found muscle and began to 'lean' into France.

The aftermath (or closing stages, depending upon viewpoint) of the Battle did not just bring welcome rest and relief for the Luftwaffe's hard pressed *Jagdgruppen*. It also saw the introduction of a new variant of their standard fighter, the Messerschmitt Bf 109. The classic *Emil*, which they

Wearing the Knight's Cross with Oak Leaves, Major Werner Mölders, *Geschwaderkommodore* of JG 51, is seen in late 1940 at the time of the *Friedrich's* introduction into service

Looking much more the part, Mölders' aircraft now sports the *Geschwader* badge on the nose, a full set of *Kommodore* markings and a rudder score in the high 60s

had flown to date, would remain in frontline service for many months to come, particularly in the southern and eastern theatres of war, but on the all-important Channel front, RAF Fighter Command found itself opposed by growing numbers of the more powerful, and aerodynamically refined Bf 109F, or *Friedrich*.

The first three Bf 109F-0 pre-production machines released for service evaluation had, in fact, been delivered to the *Stabsschwarm* of *Jagdgeschwader* 51 back at the beginning of October 1940. JG 51 was commanded by the Luftwaffe's then leading ace, 42-victory *Experte* Major Werner Mölders, who flew his first combat sortie in the *Friedrich* on 9 October. References differ, however, as to whether he was again flying one of the *Schwarm*'s trio of Bf 109F-0s when he claimed his 43rd kill (No 66 Sqn Spitfire I X4562 flown by Plt Off J H T Pickering, who bailed out wounded over Canterbury) 48 hours later.

In a somewhat superficially camouflaged blast pen made out of bales of straw, the DB 601 engine of the *Kommodore's* machine is the subject of a considerable amount of attention. This photograph was taken at Mardyck in the spring of 1941

After adding another eight victories to his score in the interim, it is on record that Mölders *was* flying *Friedrich* Wk-Nr 5628 when he despatched a brace of Spitfire Is (P7365, flown by Plt Off S F Soden, and P7309, with Plt Off P Oliver at the controls) from No 603 Sqn over Kent on 25 October. By this time, too, Hauptmann Hermann-Friedrich

Joppien's I./JG 51 was beginning to receive a few of the early Bf 109F-1 production models. It was one of these which enjoyed the dubious distinction of being the first *Friedrich* to be lost in combat when Oberleutnant Georg Claus, *Staffelkapitän* of 1./JG 51, was shot down during a Stuka escort mission on 11 November 1940. Claus, who had 18 victories to his credit, survived to become a prisoner of war. His Bf 109 F-1, Wk-Nr 5635 'White 1, went to the bottom of the Thames Estuary.

Shortly after this JG 51 was withdrawn from the Channel coast to rest and refit at two airfields in the Germany. *Geschwader* personnel were given leave at the end of December, with the pilots' enjoying a fortnight's skiing holiday in the Alps courtesy of Reichsmarschall Hermann Göring. In January 1941 ground- and aircrew met up again at Mannheim and Gütersloh, only to learn that plans for I. and IV. *Gruppen's* full conversion onto the Bf 109F had been delayed by production problems at the Messerschmitt works.

JG 51 thus returned to the Channel front still equipped predominantly with *Emils*, albeit of the latest E-7 and E-8 variants. Once arrived, Werner Mölders lost no time in resuming his friendly, but intense, rivalry with Adolf Galland, *Geschwaderkommodore* of neighbouring JG 26 (see *Osprey Aircraft of the Aces 11 - Bf 109D/E Aces 1939-41* for further details). It was perhaps indicative of the already changing tenor of cross-Channel air operations that Mölders' next victim – his first in just over ten weeks – was a Fighter Command Hurricane claimed on 10 February 1941 on the *French* side of the Channel.

Despite production bottlenecks and tardy service deliveries, two other *Jagdgeschwader* retired to Germany early in 1941 to re-equip with the *Friedrich*. The first of these was Major Günther Freiherr von Maltzahn's JG 53, the famous 'Ace-of-Spades' unit. *Stab* and all three *Gruppen*

More effectively concealed in a stand of trees, the pristine nature of this *Friedrich's Geschwader* badge, and the unblemished paintwork of its starboard undercarriage fairing and yellow undercowling, would seem to suggest that this early F-model had only recently been delivered to JG 51

The first *Friedrichs* were not without their teething problems. While the pilot (left) peers suspiciously into the bowels of his machine's engine, the mechanic at right seems more engrossed in its oil pipework

Parked outside a camouflaged hangar, this yellow-'cowlinged' Bf 109F is having its undercarriage worked on

The *Friedrich* was a formidable opponent once aloft. Here, the pilots of 'Black 7' and 'Black 9' from an unidentified III. *Gruppe* prepare for their next sortie. Note the machine just visible in the camouflaged blast pen in the background of both photos

converted onto a mix of F-1s and -2s during the course of February and March. Midway through the latter month, the first elements of the *Geschwader* returned to the Channel coast and quickly resumed combat with the RAF. In the ensuing weeks they exacted a steady toll on Fighter Command, with all but five of the 27 victories they claimed between March and early June being Spitfires.

Three pilots were credited with the lion's share of these kills. Knight's Cross holder Hauptmann Heinz Bretnütz, who had taken over command of II./JG 53 from 'Henri' Maltzahn the previous October upon the latter's elevation to *Geschwaderkommodore*, was the first to score on the *Friedrich*. The Spitfire II (of No 610 Sqn, flown by Sgt Hale) he brought down on the afternoon of 19 March took his tally to 28. He added four more kills to his total over the next two months, thereby qualifying as a *bona fide* five-victory Western front ace on the Bf 109F.

Oberfeldwebel Josef Wurmheller is seen here wearing his recently awarded Knight's Cross in front of his Bf 109F-2 in September 1941 following his posting to III./JG 2 at St Pol-Bryas

Heinz Bretnütz achieved his 33rd, and final, kill on the opening day of Operation *Barbarossa* (the German invasion of the Soviet Union), but was then himself badly wounded. His forced-landing away from base delayed immediate and life-saving medical attention, and he succumbed to his wounds in a field hospital five days later.

As the *Geschwaderkommodore* of JG 53, von Maltzahn just missed out on Western Front 'acedom' on the *Friedrich*, claiming four victories (numbers' 13 to 16) after the *Geschwader's* return to France in March 1941. But the Oberst, who was to remain in charge until October 1943, went on to greater successes in Russia and the Mediterranean.

The third member of JG 53 to achieve multiple kills flying the Bf 109F during the *Geschwader's* Channel deployment in the spring of 1941 was an up-and-coming young NCO pilot by the name of Feldwebel Josef Wurmheller. He had already achieved five victories on the *Emil*, and between 4 April and 7 May, Wurmheller added five more on the *Friedrich*. After spending a month on the Eastern front – during which time he increased his total to 19 – 'Sepp' Wurmheller was posted to III./JG 2 back on the Channel in July. Here, he would rise to become one of the foremost western *Experten* (latterly on the Fw 190 – see *Osprey Aircraft of the Aces 9 - Fw 190 Aces of the Western Front* for further details) before his death on 22 June 1944.

Jagdgeschwader 3 likewise withdrew from the Channel front early in 1941 for re-equipment with the Bf 109F. They too enjoyed the pleasures of home leave, and a skiing holiday for the pilots, as had JGs 51 and 53. Returning to France in the first week of May, they had little over a month in which to make their mark in their new mounts. But the 17 victories claimed by the *Geschwader* in that period were more than offset by an

After a brief deployment to Russia, I./JG 53 returned to Holland for the latter half of 1941. Here, they lost their *Kommandeur* over the North Sea when Hauptmann Franz von Werra's F-4 suffered engine failure off Flushing. Although not a *Friedrich* ace in the west – all 13 of von Werra's kills on the Bf 109F had been scored in Russia – he is famous as 'the one that got away', having escaped from Allied captivity in Canada after being shot down during the Battle of Britain. Seen with his pet lion cub Simba, von Werra is pictured during that earlier period of his career as the *Gruppen-Adjutant* of II./JG 3

almost equal number of pilot losses (the majority to accidental causes), with many more aircraft damaged.

Although no aces emerged from JG 3's brief period of service flying the *Friedrich* over the Channel, there were two familiar names among the individual claimants. Oberleutnant Gordon Gollob of 4./JG 3 scored his sixth victory, a Spitfire, on 7 May – after adding a further 144 kills in Russia, the highly decorated Gollob would replace the 'disgraced' Adolf Galland as *General der Jagdflieger* in January 1945. Hauptmann Walter Oesau, *Gruppenkommandeur* of III./JG 3, went one better than the future *General* by claiming two victories (a Spitfire and a Hurricane on 16 and 28 May respectively), thereby bringing his total to 42.

All three of the previously mentioned Bf 109F-equipped *Geschwader* spent relatively little time on the Channel coast prior to staging eastwards early in June 1941 in preparation for the forthcoming assault on the Soviet Union. But two other ex-Battle of Britain *Jagdgeschwader* had also enjoyed the benefits of home and Alpine leave, and subsequent re-equipment, during the early months of 1941. And when they returned to the Channel front it would be on a permanent basis – or, at least, as permanent as the exigencies of war would allow.

As the Luftwaffe's two most senior fighter units, JG 2 'Richthofen' and JG 26 'Schlageter' had been tasked with the daylight defence of northwestern Europe. While the vast bulk of the Wehrmacht sought to fulfil the Führer's ambitions for conquest and expansion to the south and east, they alone – discounting a few minor and temporary periods of reinforcement – would be responsible for guarding Europe's western coastline from Belgium to the Biscay. It was a duty they would perform, against ever increasing odds, for three long years, and which would only come to an end with the Allied invasion of Normandy, and the general withdrawal of German forces from occupied western Europe.

Initially, however, the two *Geschwader* were more than able to hold their own. Despite Fighter Command's introduction of the improved

Their yellow rudders gleaming brightly in the spring sunshine, these *Friedrichs* are almost certainly from III./JG 26 (and were therefore presumably photographed at St Brieuc). Note that compared to 'Black 7' and 'Black 9', depicted on page nine, the vertical III. *Gruppe* bar on these machines is placed close behind the fuselage cross – a characteristic of III./JG 26 during this period

As well as displaying its *Gruppe* bar 'close alongside', this F-2 – the mount of III./JG 26's *Kommandeur*, Hauptmann Gerhard Schöpfel – also wears very modestly dimensioned *Stab* chevrons. It is pictured after the *Gruppe's* transfer to Liegescourt in June 1941 . . .

Spitfire Mk V (see *Osprey Aircraft of the Aces 16 - Spitfire Mk V Aces 1941-45* for further details), it was the *Jagdwaffe's* Bf 109Fs which could usually dictate terms and decide whether or not to engage any incoming enemy formation.

The RAF's 'lean into France' was composed of specific types of operations, each with its own code-name. For example, a 'Circus' comprised a small force of bombers with a large fighter escort. Such incursions usually succeeded in their primary objective, which was to draw the

Jagdwaffe into combat. Charged with protecting key industrial and military targets, JGs 2 and 26 could ill afford to let bombers, however few in number, parade at will over areas they were responsible for defending.

'Rhubarbs' and 'Rodeos', on the other hand, which were purely fighter sweeps in small or large numbers respectively (somewhat akin to the Luftwaffe's own *freie Jagd* sorties), could safely be ignored unless the attackers were actually engaged in ground-strafing.

. . . the month Gerhard Schöpfel scored four victories, including this No 303 (Polish) Sqn Spitfire II (P8346), flown by Plt Off J Bondar. Up from Northolt as part of Circus 26, the Polish pilot was killed in the action, which took place south-east of Calais early on the morning of 28 June

Gruppenkommandeur of II./JG 2 'Richthofen', Hauptmann Karlheinz 'Heino' Greisert is shown here in the centre wearing the leather flying suit and inflatable life-jacket. Note the larger command chevrons on his aircraft, ahead of which may be seen the circular hinged panel giving access to the fuel filler cap (situated below the cockpit sill on the Bf 109F)

Another benefit enjoyed by the defending fighters was that it was now *they* who were operating over 'friendly' territory. Should a *Friedrich* be damaged and its pilot forced to bail out or crash-land, there was every likelihood that he would survive to fight another day. Some pilots bailed out so many times that they quipped they had made enough jumps to qualify for a paratrooper's badge!

The Channel *Jagdgeschwader* would gain more of an upper hand with the advent of the Focke-Wulf Fw 190. II./JG 26 began conversion on to Kurt Tank's formidable new fighter as early as August 1941, and as more *Gruppen* re-equipped, so the radial-engined Focke-Wulf would gradually supplant the *Friedrichs* in numbers and importance. But JGs 2 and 26 would both retain Messerschmitts on strength – in the form of the later Bf 109G, or *Gustav* – right up until their final retirement from France in the summer of 1944.

But let us return to spring 1941, and the early days of the Bf 109F. Neither *Geschwader* had re-equipped completely with the new model, each at first operating a mix of Fs and late-model Es. Adolf Galland of JG 26 (who had both types at his disposal – one of a *Kommodore's* little perks!) was an early and successful convert to the *Friedrich*. Having flown the type for the first time on the morning of 15 April, Galland had been invited to attend the 49th birthday celebrations of Generalmajor Theo Osterkamp, *Jafü* 2 at le Touquet, later that same afternoon.

Galland 'packed a huge basket of lobsters with the necessary bottles of champagne' into his new Bf 109F and took off from Brest-Guipavas, accompanied by his wingman. En route eastwards along the Channel he could not resist a 'little detour to pay a visit to England' – it was not the first time the *Kommodore* had made an unofficial excursion of this kind, for 11 days earlier he had done the same in his *Emil*, 'bagging' an unwary Sgt Jackie Mann (himself an ace with five kills) of No 91 Sqn in Spitfire II P7783. On the 15th he claimed two Spitfires, before continuing on his

Staffelkapitän of 7./JG 2 at St Pol-Bryas in August 1941 was Leutnant Egon Mayer. One of the true greats of the Channel front, he had risen to the rank of *Kommodore* of JG 2 and scored 102 kills by the time of his death in March 1944. Here, Mayer's 'White 1' displays the *Staffel* badge (a thumb pressing down a top hat) in miniature on the metal pennant affixed to his aerial mast, plus a generous amount of black paint above the wingroot to disguise 'those unsightly exhaust stains'

Mölders' arch-rival during the early Channel front days was Oberstleutnant Adolf Galland, *Kommodore* of JG 26 'Schlageter'. Third from left among this group of officers, the figure of Galland is unmistakable – the typical relaxed pose, the battered peaked cap, zippered leather flying trousers and boots worn with a uniform jacket, and – of course – the omnipresent cigar clutched in his left hand

way to Le Touquet, and 'Onkel Theo's' birthday party.

Galland had, in fact, shot down three Spitfire IIs, but did not claim the third, as he did not witness its destruction – all three aircraft were from No 266 Sqn, and they crash-landed at Manston (Wg Cdr W E Coope in P7901), Hawkinge (Sgt Whewell in P8014) and Hornchurch (Sgt R G V Barraclough in P7544) respectively. All three Spitfires were later repaired and returned to service.

Had Galland known that he had 'downed' all three aircraft, it would have brought his acknowledged score to 62. But he would still have been one behind his arch-rival Werner Mölders, who got his 63rd kill – he claimed that it was a 'Spitfire', although it was actually a Hurricane II of No 615 Sqn – over Boulogne that same day.

OFFENSIVE

The RAF's so-called 'non-stop' summer offensive really got underway on 14 June 1941 with Circus No 12, centred around a raid by ten Blenheims on St Omer. It heralded a period of intense activity for JGs 2 and 26, whose pilots were sometimes flying as many as five sorties a day, often against enemy formations five or ten times their own number. But it was also a period which provided ample opportunity for many *Experten*, current and future, to add significantly to their scores.

Alerted by radar, and making full use of the *Friedrich's* superior performance, the defenders would climb high to await the raiders' arrival. The RAF was at a severe disadvantage, having to fly into the sun while heading south to gain their targets, and then withdrawing with the sun now at their backs. Either way, the Messerschmitts were all but invisible as they dived out of the orb of the sun, making one slashing pass and giving the more manoeuvrable Spitfire escort little opportunity to embroil them in a dogfight.

This was exactly what Adolf Galland did one week later, on 21 June, when he shot two Blenheim IVs (from No 21 Sqn) out of another formation intent on attacking St Omer. During the second pass, however, the *Kommodore's* own machine was damaged, and he had to belly-land away from base. This did not prevent him being aloft again some four hours later, and engaging a formation of Spitfires near Boulogne. He downed one of the RAF fighters (Mk II P7730 of No 616 Sqn, flown by Plt Off E P S Brown), but was again hit himself, this time more seriously. Galland took to his parachute, having been slightly wounded by splinters.

This Spitfire had been Adolf Galland's 70th victory. During that evening's celebrations, the *Kommodore* was informed that he was the first member of the entire German armed forces to be awarded the newly-instituted highest award for bravery – the Swords to his Knight's Cross with Oak Leaves. It was a sweet moment. Werner Mölders had beaten him to the Oak Leaves by just four days the previous September. Now the positions were reversed. The announcement of the award of the Swords to Mölders came 24 hours later on the opening day of the invasion of the Soviet Union, and after he had added four more kills to the 68 he had previously scored in the west.

But the summer of 1941 did not constitute an unbroken string of successes for the two Channel-based *Jagdgeschwader*. The unrelenting pressure exerted by the RAF's offensive inevitably led to casualties too, and on 23 June 9./JG 2 was all but wiped out in action against British fighters. Casualties included the *Kapitän*, Oberleutnant Röders, and the *Staffel* had to be rebuilt almost from scratch.

JG 26 also lost three *Staffelkapitäne* in the space of just over a fortnight. And not all were as a direct result of enemy action, for the sleek lines of the *Friedrich* had been structurally suspect from the start. The early production hold-ups with the F-1 had been occasioned by the need to strengthen the unbraced tailplane, and now the rigours of combat were throwing suspicion on the integrity of the wing. On 28 June Oberleutnant Gustav Sprick, *Kapitän* of 8./JG 26, Knight's Cross holder and 31-victory *Experte*, was killed when the starboard wing of his F-2 collapsed during combat.

Five days later JG 2 suffered an even greater loss. 7./JG 27's Wilhelm Balthasar had been the most successful pilot to emerge from the *Blitzkrieg* against France. On 16 February 1941 he had replaced caretaker Karlheinz Greisert as *Kommodore* of JG 2 'Richthofen'. Having received the Knight's Cross in June 1940, he was awarded the Oak Leaves (for 40 kills) on 2 July 1941. The following day he died in similar circumstances to 'Micky' Sprick, the wing of his F-4 reportedly shearing off when he attempted an evasive spiral dive manoeuvre during combat with Spitfires.

Posthumously promoted to major, Wilhelm Balthasar was laid to rest in a World War 1 cemetery in Flanders alongside his father, who had fallen in that earlier conflict. His place at the head of JG 2 was immediately taken by Hauptmann Walter Oesau, who had been hastily recalled from his brief stint in Russia as *Gruppenkommandeur* of III./JG 3. Oesau introduced himself to the *Geschwader* with these words;

'In the spirit of Manfred von Richthofen, and following the example set by my predecessors, Major Wick and Hauptmann Balthasar, constant readiness and devotion to duty will enable us to achieve yet further successes.'

And indeed, just four days later, on 8 July 1941, the OKW was able to announce that the *Jagdgeschwader* 'Richthofen' had scored a total of 644 victories, thus equalling the record set by its World War 1 namesake. Among the victors that day was Oberleutnant Siegfried Schnell, *Staffelkapitän* of 9./JG 2,

Arguably the most prominent victim of the early *Friedrichs*' propensity to come apart in the air was Hauptmann Wilhelm Balthasar, *Geschwaderkommodore* of JG 2. Pictured here in one of the units earlier *Emils* (note the 'R' for Richthofen badge beneath the windshield), Balthasar was killed when the wing of his F-4 (Wk-Nr 7066) broke off during a dogfight with Spitfires near Aire on 3 July 1941

Oberleutnant Siegfried Schnell, *Staffelkapitän* of 9./JG 2, is seen wearing his Knight's Cross with the Oak Leaves awarded for his 40th kill on 8 July 1941

Schnell surveys his rudder, crammed to the edges with at least 49 individual kill bars. He appears to be pondering . . .

. . . was he perhaps deciding to change to this increasingly popular style of score-keeping – a painting of his decoration, with the figure 40 denoting the number of kills which had won it, plus additional individual kill bars. This rudder, showing 57 victories, was photographed at Théville at the end of May 1942. Schnell's next four successes (nos 58-61) would all be scored on 3 June – and would be recorded on the rudder of his brand new Fw 190 (see *Osprey Aircraft of the Aces 9 - Fw 190 Aces on the Western Front* for further details)

whose three kills took his score to 40, and earned him the Oak Leaves. Later, whilst flying the Fw 190, 'Wumm' Schnell would become one of the most successful Channel-based *Experten*, amassing 87 victories in the west, before taking command of IV./JG 54 on the Russian Front early in 1944.

On 10 July the RAF was presented with an almost intact *Friedrich*. On that date the target for Circus No 42's bombers – a trio of Stirlings – was Chocques power station, in northern France. One of the bombers was shot down over the Continent (falling victim either to flak or an RAF fighter – reports are conflicting), while another, already damaged, was followed back across the Channel by Hauptmann Rolf Pingel, *Gruppenkommandeur* of I./JG 26.

Pingel, a Knight's Cross holder with 22 victories to his credit, plus another four scored earlier in Spain with the *Condor Legion*, later described what happened next;

'I followed one of the *dicken Brummer* ('fat buzzers') as it made its way back to England, and hoped to be able to carry out an attack. But then I was hit. Whether by one of its gunners or by an English fighter, I don't know. Perhaps both. My engine started to run unevenly, and oil and coolant temperatures began to climb.

'I tried to escape close to the ground, as I had done many times before. There were many English machines in the air around Dover. While still at low-level my engine came to an almost complete stop. Unable to bail out, I had no other choice but to belly-land.'

Pingel came down in a cornfield just off the Dover-Deal road. He immediately tried to set fire to his machine, but was dissuaded from doing so by a group of British soldiers hurrying to the scene, who aimed a burst of machine-gun fire over his head.

Hauptmann Rolf Pingel, *Gruppen-kommandeur* of I./JG 26, poses in front of his earlier *Emil* (note the 87 octane fuel triangle above Pingel's left shoulder for the dorsal filler cap)

And the similarly marked *Friedrich* in which he made a forced landing near Dover on 10 July 1941

The tail of Pingel's F-2 displays his 22 World War 2 kills, the first 10 of which were gained while serving as *Staffelkapitän* of 2./JG 53, and the last dozen as *Kommandeur* of I./JG 2 – he had earlier scored four in Spain with the *Condor Legion*. Note also the stiffeners above the tailwheel leg where the aft fuselage frame (no 9) is attached to the notoriously weak tail unit

Perhaps caught at a wrong moment, an unusually sombre Oberleutnant Josef Priller, *Staffelkapitän* of 1./JG 26, peers grumpily from the cockpit of his F-4 as a groundcrewman helps him prepare for his next sortie from St Omer-Clairmarais sometime in the latter half of 1941. Soon to be exchanged for an Fw 190, this *Friedrich* – like all 'Pips' Priller's aircraft – carries his personal insignia below the cockpit: an ace-of-hearts bearing his wife's name *Jutta*

His Bf 109F-2, Wk-Nr 12764, was quickly repaired and subsequently test-flown (as ES906) in mock combat with RAF fighters until it was written off in a fatal crash on 20 October 1941 – its pilot, Flg Off M Skalski, of the Air Fighting Development Unit, was overcome by carbon monoxide during a flight from Fowlmere, in Cambridgeshire.

A lot of new data on the *Friedrich* was gathered prior to the fighter's early demise, although Pingel, himself, yielded little beyond name, rank and serial number. But a preliminary interrogation adjudged his morale to be 'very high', and reported that 'this pilot is held in high esteem by all fighter pilots, and has undoubtedly done a great deal to raise and maintain the morale and the *esprit-de-corps* of JG 26, the "Galland *Geschwader*"'. A further snippet was gleaned from the R/T codes in the aircraft, which confirmed JG 26's current call-signs as the names of European rivers – 'Fulda' for the Stab, 'Moldau' for I. and 'Isar' for II./JG 26.

Four days after Pingel's capture, one of his erstwhile *Staffelkapitäne* claimed his 40th kill (a Spitfire south of Dunkirk), for which he would be

The award of the Knight's Cross to three members of JG 2 'Richthofen' on 1 August 1941 was a major event, and the subject of much news coverage. Here, the recently decorated trio, together with their CO, are photographed for a Berlin newspaper as they stroll past a *Friedrich* of the *Stabsschwarm*. They are, from left to right, Leutnant Egon Mayer (*Staffelkapitän* of 7./JG 2), Oberleutnant Rudolf Pflanz (*Geschwader-TO*), *Kommodore* Major Walter Oesau and Oberleutnant Erich Leie (*Geschwader*-Adjutant)

awarded the Oak Leaves on 20 July. Oberleutnant Josef Priller had led 1./JG 26 since November 1940. Soon to convert to Fw 190s upon his promotion to *Kommandeur* of III./JG 26, 'Pips' Priller, a diminutive 'perennially smiling' Bavarian, would emerge as one of the outstanding personalities of the Channel Front, and one of the very few *Jagdflieger* to score more than 100 kills against the Western allies.

Where markings were concerned, the *Stabsschwarm* of JG 2 was a law unto itself. Major Oesau's aircraft carried the standard pre-war *Geschwaderkommodore* insignia as laid down in a Luftwaffe directive dated 2 July 1936

By the same token, the *Friedrich* of Adjutant Oberleutnant Erich Leie (pictured here later when *Kommandeur* of I./JG 2) should have carried plain horizontal bars either side of the fuselage cross. But Leie chose to add to these bars a wartime *Geschwader*-Adjutant's symbols of chevron and vertical bar to produce the unusual combination depicted in colour profile no 4

Traditionally, the third man in a *Geschwaderstabskette* was the TO, or Technical Officer. Oesau's TO was Oberleutnant Rudolf Pflanz, and he opted for the standard 'third man's' markings of horizontal bars plus a small rectangular dot . . .

19

... which may just be made out here as he explains the workings of his *Friedrich* to a visiting German nursing sister. Erich Leie is standing on the port wing. But dare one suggest, in these politically correct times, that Feldwebel Seeger, on the left, seems to be more interested in the curves beneath that starched uniform than in the intricacies of a Bf 109F-4!

By a process of elimination, the fourth member of the *Stabsschwarm*, Stabsfeldwebel Fritz Stritzel, was presumably the pilot of the curiously marked *Friedrich*, pictured here at St Pol in the late summer of 1941. Note that once again the *Stab* of JG 2 are playing host to a female visitor

In the spring of 1942 the *Stabsschwarm* transferred to Beaumont-le-Roger. The same *Friedrich* as above may now be seen behind the standard denoting *Geschwader* HQ, while the *Kommodore's* machine is beyond the tree on the far right ...

During this period lesser known names were also achieving significant successes too. On 18 July 2./JG 26's Feldwebel Ernst Jäckel was credited with the destruction of the first four-engined bomber to be shot down by a Luftwaffe day fighter, his victim being a No 15 Sqn Stirling which crashed into the sea off the Kent coast. Five days later Oberleutnant Rudolf Pflanz, a long-serving member of JG 2, claimed a remarkable six British aircraft in a single day. Fighter Command lost no fewer than 22

... by this time, however, Major Oesau had been banned from further combat flying, and his aircraft was 'officially' to be used for non-operational purposes only. To make up the *Stabsschwarm*'s numbers when flying operational sorties a new fourth man was drafted in from 8. *Staffel.* And just to confuse matters, Feldwebel Josef Bigge's *Friedrich* wore the plain horizontal bars of a pre-war adjutant!

One final complication arose when the *Stabsschwarm* increased its numbers from four to six. The two new members were Leutnant Fritz Edelmann and his wingman Oberfeldwebel Carl. A photograph of the latter's aircraft has yet to be found, but Edelmann's machine sported arguably the most peculiar markings of all – the *Schwarm*'s horizontal bars fronted by half a chevron! Could this have been a tongue-in-cheek joke reflecting Edelmann's ambitions as a '*Kommodore*-in-waiting'?

Spitfires and three Hurricanes to all causes on this date. Pflanz's Knight's Cross was awarded on 1 August – the month which was to see the *Jagdgeschwader* 'Richthofen's' total tally rise to 800 victories.

Other notable events in August 1941 included the clash between the RAF's Tangmere Wing and JG 26 on the 9th, which ended the wartime flying career of the legendary legless ace Douglas Bader. Just who shot Bader down has never been positively established, but the subsequent reception accorded the British wing commander by Adolf Galland and his staff at *Geschwader* HQ in Audembert was to sow the seeds for a life-long postwar friendship between the two former adversaries.

On 14 August 1941 another irrepressible Channel Front character was awarded the Oak Leaves for passing the 40-victory mark. Despite his natural ebullience, Hauptmann Hans 'Assi' Hahn was an outstanding fighter pilot and tactician. Under his leadership, III./JG 2 became one of the most successful of the Channel-based *Jagdgruppen*. The *Kommandeur* himself was to take his score in the west to 68 – including four heavy bombers – before being posted to command II./JG 54 in Russia in late 1942.

As previously noted, one who had made the journey 'the other way' was JG 2's *Kommodore*, Major Walter Oesau, who claimed his 66th western

Also based at St Pol in August 1941 was III./JG 2 under Hauptmann Hans 'Assi' Hahn, seen here being greeted by his pet Great Dane 'Wumm'. Note the patch below the windscreen where the 'Richthofen' badge has been overpainted (in compliance with a recent western front edict prohibiting such identifiable unit emblems)

Lower-level or personal markings presumably escaped the ban – or was it simply ignored in such cases? 'Assi' Hahn's *Friedrich* proudly sports his *Gruppe's* 'cockerel's head' badge . . .

. . . seen even more clearly in this close-up of the cowling of a III./JG 2 machine

Hauptmann Hahn (right) with two of his *Staffelkapitäne*, Leutnants Bruno Stolle (left) of 8./JG 2 and Egon Mayer (centre) of 7./JG 2. Note the *Staffel* badges decorating the chalet-style dispersal hut behind the group and the even more distinctive markings of 'Wumm' in the foreground

front victory on 26 October 1941 (Spitfire VB AB822 of No 72 Sqn, flown by Sgt L Stock). This brought his total score to 100. He was the third member of the *Jagdwaffe* to reach the 'century' mark, beaten only by Mölders and Lützow (the former now taken off combat flying and appointed as the first *General der Jagdflieger*, and the latter still commanding JG 3 in the east).

23

The *Gruppe 'Spiess'* (senior NCO, somewhat akin to 'Chiefy' in the RAF) supervises the return of a III./JG 2 *Friedrich* into its small wooden hangar . . .

. . . all neat and tidy. Just as 'Chiefies' the world over – whatever their uniform – like things to be!

Walter Oesau, pictured in typically casual attire, during the celebrations marking his 100th victory. He was the third fighter pilot in the world to achieve the 'century'

But arguably the brightest star in the Channel firmament during the late summer and early autumn of 1941 was Austrian Johann Schmid. Having already claimed nine Battle of Britain kills as a member of JG 2, Oberleutnant Schmid joined JG 26 in July 1941, initially flying with Galland's *Stabsschwarm*. In less than a month his score had risen to 25 – including three RAF fighters on each of three separate days between 7 and 10 August – for which he was duly awarded the Knight's Cross. He was also promoted to Hauptmann and given command of 8. *Staffel*.

Schmid's 45th, and final, victim was a Spitfire (almost certainly a Mk VB of No 452 Sqn, RAAF, flown by Sgt B M Geissman), which he shot into the Channel off Calais on 6 November. Circling the point of impact at very low level, Schmid's wingtip hit the surface of the water and the

Friedrich also disappeared beneath the waves.

Two days after the loss of Hauptmann Schmid, the disastrous, and costly (17 Spitfires were lost) Circus No 110, targeted at Lille, finally brought the curtain down on the RAF's 'non-stop' offensive of 1941. But Fighter Command continued to mount cross-Channel sweeps despite the worsening weather. By this time Oberstleutnant Galland's score was nearing the coveted 'century'. On 18 November he claimed what he believed to be his 96th victory (although subsequent research has suggested that his total was then

A III./JG 26 'black man' (Luftwaffe slang for groundcrew, so called because of the colour of their overalls) is seen busily engaged in removing the accumulated exhaust and oil stains before 'White 10's' next flight – note the starting handle already in place

actually standing at 94). Number 100 would remain tantalisingly out of reach for more than three long years (see *Osprey Aircraft of the Aces 17 - German Jet Aces of World War 2* for further details).

TRAGIC PROMOTION

On 17 November 1941 Generaloberst Ernst Udet, the Luftwaffe's overburdened *Generalluftzeugmeister* (Chief of Aircraft Procurement and Supply) had committed suicide. Despite his shortcomings – he was held largely to blame for the Luftwaffe's 'failure' during the Battle of Britain – Udet was to be accorded a state funeral. Galland was ordered to Berlin to form part of the guard of honour, as too was Werner Mölders, who was currently on a tour of inspection of the Eastern front. It was while *en route* back to the capital that Mölders lost his life when the He 111 in which he was a passenger crashed at Breslau-Gandau. Galland was immediately appointed his successor as the new *General der Jagdflieger*.

One of the early tasks facing Galland in his new role would be to organise an effective fighter screen for Operation *Donnerkeil*. This involved the 'escape' up-Channel, via the Straits of Dover, of three capital ships of the Kriegsmarine (the battlecruisers *Scharnhorst* and *Gneisenau,* and the heavy cruiser *Prinz Eugen*) from Brest in western France – where they had been holed up for months, protected by elements of JG 2 – to the relative safety of German home waters.

Galland's plan for the provision of an uninterrupted fighter umbrella to cover the naval force as it raced eastwards hinged upon four *Führungszentralen* (command centres), which he established parallel to the ships' line of advance. Located at Caen, Le Touquet, Schiphol and Jever, these centres in turn controlled a chain of overlapping sub-sectors stretching the length of the Channel and North Sea coasts. Each sub-sector housed a fighter force which would take off and escort the flotilla as it passed through its assigned area.

Timing would be of the essence. Consecutive groups of 16 fighters (four *Schwärme*) would remain on station above the ships for exactly 30 minutes. However, every group would be joined for the last ten of those minutes by the next scheduled formation. This meant, in effect, that for half of the 'dash' there would be no fewer than 32 fighters flying wide figures of eight around the speeding flotilla. Galland also ordered his fighters to remain at low level to escape detection by British radar, and that strict radio silence was to be observed.

Although augmented by several other units, the 180 Messerschmitts and Focke-Wulfs of JGs 2 and 26 would be responsible for the ships' safety during the most hazardous stage of the voyage – the approach to, and passage through, the narrow confines of the Straits of Dover. As the more westerly of the two *Geschwader*, JG 2 would be the first on station.

Shortly before midnight on 11 February 1942, the trio of heavy ships, escorted by seven destroyers, slipped out of Brest harbour. As dawn approached, they were nearing Cherbourg. Here, they were met by a dozen E-boats, while overhead the first *Schwarm* of the day's fighter cover – four Bf 110 nightfighters, in fact, specially chosen to bridge the dangerous period of false dawn before full daylight – began their monotonous circling. As the sky lightened to the east, the twin-engined *Zerstörer* were firstly reinforced, and then replaced, by the Bf 109s of JG 2.

Tension rose throughout the morning of 12 February as each group of fighters was succeeded by the next in accordance with Galland's carefully orchestrated time-table. But there was absolutely no reaction from the British. Under lowering clouds, the flotilla ploughed its way undetected and unopposed across the Bay of the Seine, its course – east by north-east – taking it steadily closer to the Straits of Dover.

Incredibly, through a series of mishaps and misunderstandings (and aided in no small measure by the Germans' jamming of their coastal radar), the British High Command remained unaware of the flotilla's progress until it was about to negotiate the straits. Their first response – a salvo from the Dover shore batteries at 1316 hours – was ineffectual. So too was the first aerial attack, mounted some 18 minutes later by half-a-dozen antiquated Swordfish torpedo-bombers of the Fleet Air Arm's 825 Naval Air Squadron (NAS), escorted by No 72 Sqn's Spitfire Vs (a total of five Spitfire squadrons were supposed to support the Swordfish, but the remainder never showed up).

This western-based F-4 taxiing along a perimeter track is fitted with a standard 300-litre (66-gal) external drop tank, which presumably indicates that it is about to take-off on a long overwater patrol. As frequently happened, the front of the tank has been covered in a thin film of oil caused by a slight leak in the system above. This has led in the past to such tanks being mistakenly described as 'having a transparent nose cone'

Operating from Manston, the vulnerable biplanes stood no chance at all. Just as they were approaching the ships, JG 2's protective screen of Bf 109s was joined by Focke-Wulfs of III./JG 26. Between them, the German fighters shot all six of the Swordfish into the sea. The strength of the attacking force, whose leader, Lt Cdr Eugene Esmonde, would be awarded a posthumous Victoria Cross, was grossly overestimated by the defenders. Post-action reports credited JG 2 with the destruction of seven Swordfish, JG 26's Fw 190s with three, and the ships' flak gunners with a further six!

This engagement, which had taken place between Calais and Dunkirk – well within JG 26's area of operations – did not mean the end of the day's activities for JG 2. Just as *Schwärme* of JG 26 had earlier been deployed to the west to supplement JG 2's numbers, so now Bf 109s of JG 2 'leap-frogged' eastwards to help further protect the ships as they traversed JG 26's sub-sectors.

Their assistance would be welcome. Fifteen minutes after the sacrificial Swordfish strike, Galland gave the order lifting radio silence, and for the next three hours and more, penny-packet formations of British bombers and fighter-bombers would brave the worsening weather in desperate attempts to cripple the three cruisers, but to no avail.

By the time the German flotilla departed their areas, JG 2 had claimed 20 British aircraft without loss to themselves and JG 26 a more modest seven. The latter lost four of their own, including a *Friedrich* of I. *Gruppe*. The final confrontations of the day took place in the late afternoon off the Dutch coast when fighters of JG 1 accounted for seven RAF bombers. Galland's plan had worked to perfection, for the Kriegsmarine's ships had survived every air attack completely unscathed. The only crumb of comfort for the RAF was the damage both battlecruisers had suffered from

After the successful conclusion of the 'Channel Dash', Major Walter Oesau chose to return from Brest by road with the ground party. He is seen here arriving back at Beaumont-le-Roger in his Luftwaffe-registered Hotchkiss open-top tourer, complete with miniature *Geschwaderkommodore* flags

mines laid earlier off the Frisian Islands. But in neither case was this serious, serving only to slightly delay the ships' arrival in German ports.

Although he had been succeeded at the head of JG 26 by the very able Major Gerhard Schöpfel, previously the *Kommandeur* of III. *Gruppe*, Galland's unwilling departure for his desk job in Berlin, and his subsequent organisation of the aerial component of the 'Channel Dash' (in his own words, admittedly his 'finest hour'), marked the close of an era on the Channel front. For the brief reign of the *Friedrich* in the west was about to come to an end as both JGs 2 and 26 began to convert completely onto the Fw 190. Throughout 1942 the two *Geschwader* would continue to defend their respective sectors of the coast – JG 2 the Biscay and the Channel 'from Brest to the Somme', and JG 26 the Pas de Calais and Belgium – against growing pressure from the western allies. But by the time of the next major cross-Channel operation of 1942 (the ill-starred Canadian landings at Dieppe in August) all six component *Gruppen* of the two *Jagdgeschwader* would be flying the Fw 190.

Before that, however, JG 2's *Friedrichs* had been involved in one other action of note. This was another British attack which would be distinguished by the award of the Victoria Cross to its leader. This time the target was not a flotilla of ships at sea, but the MAN diesel engine workshops at Augsburg, in Bavaria, some 450 miles (725 km) inland. And the attacking force was not made up of a clutch of 'stick-and-string' biplanes, but a dozen of the RAF's new four-engined Lancaster bombers.

But there were *some* similarities between this operation (an experimental raid aimed at taking out a pin-point target deep in enemy territory) and that launched against the battlecruisers two months earlier – it would be flown in daylight and at low level!

The 12 Lancasters, of Nos 44 and 97 Sqns, led by South African Sqn Ldr J D Nettleton, took off in the mid-afternoon of 17 April 1942. Although historians have since claimed that the diversionary sweeps over northern France laid on at the same time 'served to alert rather than distract' the defenders, JG 2 seem to have been taken completely by surprise as Nettleton, and the leading wave of six Lancasters, roared low over their main base. Otto Happel remembered it vividly;

'It was late in the afternoon of 17 April at Beaumont le Roger. Our fighters had been up on their last operation of the day, and the first of them were just returning and coming in to land when somebody yelled: "*Viermots* flying low over the field!"

'I immediately warned our incoming fighters over the R/T of the danger. Major Walter Oesau shot past me like greased lightning, heading for his Me 109 which was always held at instant readiness. Without further ado he set off after the departing bombers.'

There was a long running fight between the Luftwaffe fighters and the Lancasters which lasted a full hour. Otto Happel again;

'We later learned that four of the bombers had been shot down. Unteroffizier Pohl's victim was the *Geschwader's* 1000th kill, and Major Oesau's the 1001st (the latter, No 44 Sqn's L7536/KM-H, which was only the tenth production Lancaster to be built, came down near Bernay, taking Oesau's own score to 101).

'It was common knowledge that *Kommodore* Oesau had received *Startverbot* (i.e. had been banned from operational flying after achieving his 'century' the previous October), but his excuse was a classic. He immediately informed his superiors that he had been up on a routine test flight when these monsters suddenly appeared out of nowhere and he had been forced to shoot down a Lancaster purely out of self-defence. A perfectly believable story to anybody who did not know the true facts.'

Oesau's *Stabskette* would be among the last in JG 2 to relinquish their Bf 109Fs (in August). Unlike many fighter pilots, who regarded the *Friedrich* with its single cannon (plus two fuselage machine-guns) as undergunned, the *Kommodore* himself was obviously a devotee. Both JGs 2 and 26 did retain a dozen or so specialised F-4/R1s on strength during the spring and early summer of 1942, these equipping the *Geschwader's* two fighter-bomber *Staffeln*, which had been activated in February-March of that year.

JABO 'HUNTERS'

By the very nature of their calling, the pilots of the *Jabostaffeln* were hardly likely to become aces. Their targets were Channel shipping and shore installations along the southern coast of England, and they proved very successful in this role – Hauptmann Frank Liesendahl's 10.(*Jabo*)/JG 2, for example, claimed to have sunk 20 ships totalling some 63,000 BRT, between March and June. Hauptmann Karl Plunser's 10.(*Jabo*)/JG 26 appear, initially at least, to have concentrated more on land targets. This *Staffel* reportedly flew its first operation over England on 19 April 1942. Five days later they suffered their first loss when Feldwebel Hans-Jürgen Fröhlich, who had scored five kills during his earlier service with 2. *Staffel*, was hit by anti-aircraft fire after bombing a Folkestone gasometer.

Both *Staffelkapitäne* were also to fall victim to anti-aircraft fire in July, by which time re-equipment with the Fw 109A-3 had taken place. The veteran Liesendahl of 10.(*Jabo*)/JG 2 was killed attacking a tanker off Brixham on the 17th. Oberleutnant Hans-Joachim Geburtig, who had been at the head of 10.(*Jabo*)/JG 26 for less than a fortnight, was likewise brought down by a collier off Littlehampton on 30 July, but survived to become a prisoner-of-war.

Almost concurrent with their *Jabostaffeln's* conversion to Fw 190s, the two Channel-based *Jagdgeschwader* each activated an 11. *Staffel*. These new units were specifically intended for high-altitude operations and, as

Hauptmann Liesendahl's F-4/B 'Blue 1' (Wk-Nr 7629) pictured on the wide expanse of Beaumont-le-Roger in the spring of 1942

such, were equipped with the first production models of the latest addition to the prolific Messerschmitt family, the *Gustav* – the pressurised Bf 109G-1.

The officer selected to command 11./JG 2 was a long-serving member of the *Geschwader*, who had flown in the *Stabsschwarm* with both Wick and Oesau. Recently, Oberleutnant Rudolf Pflanz (one of the most successful pilots currently flying on the Channel front) had given up his post of *Geschwader* TO (Technical

Officer) to take over at the head of 1./JG 2 – the unit which then provided the cadre for the new high-altitude *Staffel*. Based first at St Pol, and later transferring to Poix, 11./JG 2's task was to combat the RAF Spitfires flying top cover for the growing number of bombing raids which were again being despatched against northern France. It was during one such engagement, against Circus No 201 on 31 July, that Oberleutnant Pflanz was to lose his life.

. . . and a detailed shot of Frank Liesendahl's personal scoreboard showing six freighters – ranging from 2500 to 10,000 BRT – sunk or damaged to varying degrees, the last of which is dated '31.3.42'. It was after attacking another such freighter off Brixham on 17 July 1942 that Hauptmann Liesendahl was reported missing

Whereas 10.(*Jabo*)/JG 2 sported both a *Staffel* badge and special *Jabo* insignia (the chevron and bar behind the fuselage cross), the F-4/Bs of 10.(*Jabo*)/JG 26 based along the coast at St Omer-Arques combined the two with a 'falling bomb' emblem on their rear fuselages. Here 'White 9' begins her take-off run. Note the armoured windshield, and the minimal ground clearance for the 250-kg (550-lb) bomb

Having claimed his 51st kill on 30 July, Pflanz led his *Staffel* aloft again 24 hours later to contest the next RAF incursion. References differ as to the exact course of the subsequent action north of Abbeville as the Messerschmitts became split up in heavy fighting against several squadrons of Spitfire VBs. One thing is clear, however. The leader had unknowingly lost his wingman. Some sources indicate that Feldwebel Heinz Grüber had baled out wounded after his *Gustav* was hit, whilst others state that he managed to crash-land at Etaples.

Unaware that his tail was uncovered, Oberleutnant Pflanz had just achieved his 52nd, and last, victory (another Spitfire) when his own machine was mortally hit. Again references diverge. One source describes Pflanz's aircraft as 'exploding in mid-air', but Gefreiter Hieronymus of *Stab* JG 2 reports that the *Staffelkapitän* was unable to release the damaged canopy from the pressurised cockpit. Despite the uncertainty of the circumstances leading up to its loss, the wreckage of Pflanz's stricken *Gustav* (Wk-Nr 10318) was found in sand dunes some seven miles (12 km) south of Berck-sur-Mer, where it had impacted at precisely 1505 hours. Command of 11./JG 2 immediately passed to Oberleutnant Julius Meimberg, who would lead the *Staffel* until its departure for the Mediterranean in November.

The brief history of JG 26's Channel-based high-altitude *Staffel* paralleled that of JG 2. Formed late in July 1942 from a nucleus provided by I. *Gruppe*, 11./JG 26's first *Staffelkapitän* was nine-victory Oberleutnant Johannes Schmidt, erstwhile leader of 3. *Staffel*. Schmidt quickly took his score into double figures with the destruction of a Spitfire on 30 July. Nearly three weeks were to pass before his next, and final, successes – a pair of Spitfires brought down during the opening hours of the Dieppe

Sister-ship 'White 11' did not make it back to St Omer after an attack on a Royal Navy corvette off Newhaven on 20 May 1942. His aircraft hit by return fire, pilot Unteroffizier Oswald Fischer was forced to belly land on Beachy Head. Only slightly damaged, Wk-Nr 7232 was later test flown – minus her mangled bomb-rack – by the RAF as NN644 from October 1943 until war's end. Altogether, some two-dozen fighters and fighter-bombers of JGs 2 and 26 were brought down over or near the UK in 1942. But many more RAF machines failed to return from cross-Channel operations over occupied northern Europe, which is hardly surprising, given the numbers involved. Although the exact reason for their demise is not known, the following are representative of the opposition faced by the Luftwaffe's two western-based *Jagdgeschwader* . . .

. . . the wreckage of Spitfire VB BM329 of No 122 'Bombay' Sqn, which crashed in dunes near Boulogne during a 'Rhubarb' (fighter sweep) on 15 July 1942 after being struck by flak. Its pilot, Sgt D S James, was killed in the crash. Two other Spitfire pilots lost their lives during this large-scale 'Rhubarb' as a result of deadly flak – No 154 Sqn's Flt Sgt A R Bray (in BM486), and then ranking RAF ace Wg Cdr Brendan 'Paddy' Finucane (in No 154 Sqn's BM308), who was the Hornchurch Wing Leader at the time

Another Spitfire VB, which came to grief in a cornfield. Part of No 306 'Torun' Sqn, this aircraft was almost certainly the fighter flown by Polish pilot Plt Off C Daszuta, who failed to return from Circus 95 (just one of nine Mk VBs lost during this operation) on 17 September 1941. Daszuta spent the rest of the war as a PoW

Army co-op Mustang I AG585 of No 239 Sqn was photographed with its nose buried in a French copse. This particular aircraft is the only one of the three downed RAF fighters seen on this page to show visible signs of combat damage – even if it is just a single bullet hole above the tailfin flash!

landings on 19 August. Shortly thereafter Schmidt became caught up in a low-level dogfight which ended with the high-altitude *Gustav's* crashing into the sea.

The only other member of 11./JG 26 to score over Dieppe that day was Oberfeldwebel Emil Babenz, an experienced NCO pilot whom Schmidt had brought with him from 3. *Staffel*. The three Spitfires he claimed raised Babenz's total to 21. Although Babenz was undoubtedly 11./JG 26's most successful pilot, the newly-vacant position of *Staffelkapitän* required commissioned rank, so III. *Gruppe's* Oberleutnant Hans-Jürgen Westphal was duly appointed to the post. Like 'Jule' Meimberg of neighbouring 11./JG 2, Westphal would remain in office until 11./JG 26's transfer to the Mediterranean theatre in November.

The departure of the two high-altitude *Staffeln* for sunnier climes (and subsequent incorporation into other units) did not mark the end of JGs 2 and 26's association with the Bf 109. By the early autumn of 1942, a menacing new dimension had been added to the cross-Channel air war – the embryonic US Eighth Air Force. It was over northern France that the first small-scale raids by B-17 and B-24 heavy bombers were carried out.

The Luftwaffe High Command was not slow to realise the incipient threat posed by these early attacks by the high-flying 'heavies', and their even higher (albeit as yet still short-ranged) fighter escorts. The rugged and hard-hitting Fw 190s which currently equipped the two Channel-based *Jagdgeschwader* were ideal anti-bomber gun platforms. But the Focke-Wulf's performance degraded sharply at altitude. What was needed to supplement the Fw 190 was a machine designed expressly for the fighter role. And just such an aircraft was about to enter service – the Bf 109G-4. It was therefore decided that JGs 2 and 26 would henceforth operate a mix of Fw 190s and the new *Gustavs*.

Before 1942 was out, both II. and III./JG 26 were being thus equipped. Whether the powers-that-be were swayed by the former's undisguised lack of enthusiasm at having to give up their trusty Focke-Wulfs for the latest Messerschmitt is open to question. But, for whatever reason, it was III./JG 26 who were finally chosen to convert back entirely on to the Bf 109. From 1943 until the closing months of the war, they were the only *Gruppe* of JG 26 to operate successive models of the *Gustav*. After a brief flirtation with the Bf 109K late in 1944, III./JG 26 finally came into line with the rest of the *Geschwader* again when they were re-equipped with the 'long nose' Fw 190D-9.

JG 2 followed a similar pattern. Initially both I. and II. *Gruppen* operated the two types of fighter alongside each other, but it would ultimately fall to II./JG 2 to re-equip completely with the new Bf 109G-6 after their return from service in Tunisia in the late spring of 1943. They too would be the

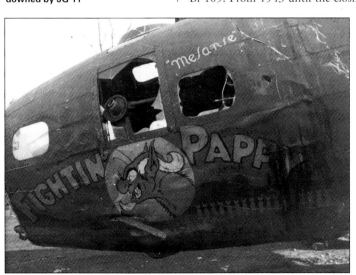

The new enemy – B-17F 42-5407 was an aircraft of the 306th BG ('the oldest operational bomb group of the Eighth AF), which flew its first mission, against Lille, on 9 October 1942. Living a charmed life, this Fortress subsequently served with both the 91st and 379th BGs before its luck finally ran out near Kiel on 9 October 1943. It was probably downed by JG 11

33

only *Gruppe* in their *Geschwader* to revert to, and retain, Bf 109s until almost the end of the war, when they too received the Fw 109D-9.

Throughout 1943 and the early months of 1944, while still expected to contest the RAF's sweeps into north-west European airspace, the Messerschmitts of II./JG 2 and III./JG 26 would find themselves increasingly involved in the fight against the US 'heavies'. In effect, they formed the first line of defence in what was developing into the Battle of the Reich.

NORTH SEA TRIANGLE

The earlier mention, in passing, of JG 1's participation in the closing stages of the 'Channel Dash' serves to introduce the third *Jagdgeschwader* involved in the defence of the north-western continental seaboard. Deployed on JG 26's right flank, JG 1's areas of responsibility initially covered the Dutch and German North Sea coastal sectors. Since the Battle of the German Bight in late 1939, which had seen a heterogeneous force of Luftwaffe fighters severely maul a formation of attacking RAF Wellingtons (see *Osprey Aircraft of the Aces 11* and *25* for further details), the lower shores of the North Sea had become something of a backwater.

For a year Oberleutnant Carl Schumacher's *Stab* JG 1, which had no component *Gruppen* of its own (the original, semi-autonomous I./JG 1 never operated as part of Schumacher's command, being redesignated III./JG 27 in July 1940), controlled a transient miscellany of units – either on their way to, or resting from, service on other fronts – in defence of the region. It was not until December 1940 that the first move was made towards establishing a JG 1 proper by the activation of a 1. *Staffel.*

Nine more months were to pass before I./JG 1 existed in its entirety under the command of World War I veteran Major Dr Erich Mix, by which time the *Gruppe* had begun to receive its first *Friedrichs*. Paucity of targets prevented full use being made of the new fighter, and in the last half of 1941 I./JG 1's *Staffeln* claimed just eight kills between them, all but two of their victims being twin-engined Blenheims.

A sudden flurry of activity early in 1942 saw the creation of no fewer than three new *Gruppen*:II,/JG 1 was formed by the simple expedient of redesignating the Bf 109F-equipped I./JG 3, recently returned from the Eastern front, and III. and IV./JG 1 were made up from reserve *Staffeln* of other *Geschwader*; the former being deployed in Denmark and southern Norway, the latter soon to be incorporated into JG 5 (whereupon a second IV./JG 1 was immediately activated, mainly from intakes fresh from fighter training schools).

Despite stiffening opposition, and a lengthening list of unit successes, 1942 failed to produce any *Friedrich* aces from within the ranks of JG 1, for during the summer months three of the *Gruppen* had begun to re-equip with the Fw 190. By the autumn only I./JG 1 was still flying Messerschmitts – and currently adding high-altitude Bf 109G-1s to its Fs and few remaining Es. But one future *Experte* and Knight's Cross recipient did open his scoreboard during this period. 2./JG 1's Leutnant Heinz Knoke claimed his first kill – a Blenheim north of the Frisian Islands – on 31 October. Six days later he despatched a Mosquito some 30 miles (50 km) north-west of Heligoland.

Arguably of greater portent were the two B-17s brought down (by pilots of II. *Gruppe* over France) on 6 December. These were the first of their kind to fall victim to JG 1, and within weeks the fight against Boeing's four-engined heavy bomber would be dominating the *Geschwader's* very existence. But the first Flying Fortress to be claimed by the Luftwaffe – in fact, the first to be lost to enemy action in World War 2 – had gone down almost exactly 15 months earlier . . . in an unlikely quarter, and to an even unlikelier opponent.

The Kriegsmarine's first aircraft carrier, the 23,200-ton *Graf Zeppelin* launched in December 1938 but was destined never to be completed. Navalised versions of the two types of aircraft intended for service aboard her – the Ju 87 and the Bf 109 – were, however, designed and produced. The Bf 109T (T=*Träger*/carrier) shipboard fighter was based upon the *Emil*, the major external difference being the T's increased wing span and the provision of catapult points and an arrestor hook.

When it became apparent that there was little likelihood of the Bf 109T ever being used in its planned role, the aircraft were 'de-navalised' and, in mid-1941, issued instead to standard Luftwaffe fighter units – many went to I./JG 77 in southern Norway. Like the original IV./JG 1 previously mentioned, I./JG 77 was soon to form part of the new JG 5. In the interim its component *Staffeln*, dispersed on airfields along Norway's western seaboard, were operating under a variety of temporary designations.

Shortly after midday on 8 September 1941, six Bf 109Ts of one such *Staffel* (the *Jagdgruppe Stavanger*), were scrambled in response to a report of approaching enemy aircraft. Leutnant Alfred Jakobi and his wingman, Leutnant Steinicke, headed southwards, and soon the former could see a pair of condensation trails high over open water, drawing west to east. The two fighters climbed towards them on an intercept course. When they were at an altitude of 8600 m (28,000 ft), the tell-tale trails, now over land, suddenly ceased. Then Jakobi spotted a black speck against the milky haze of the horizon, and it took him all of 12 minutes to overhaul it. From a distance of 400 m (450 yards) Jakobi was finally able to get a good look at his foe, which, he thought, could only be a Boeing Fortress!

The time Jakobi had spent studying the recognition manuals had obviously not been wasted, for his opponent was indeed a Fortress. A 0915 hours (local time) that morning, Fortress I AN525/WP-D of No 90 Sqn – the only RAF bomber squadron to be equipped with the four-engined

Although heavily retouched, this photo of Bf 109T (Wk-Nr 7743) does clearly show the increased wing span of this variant. Still wearing its original *Stammkennzeichen* (RB+OP), this machine subsequently served with JG 77, before ending its days with a nightfighter school

Boeing – had lifted off from Kinloss, in Scotland, in the company of three others to attack the *Panzerschiff* (pocket-battleship) *Admiral Scheer* in Oslo harbour.

As the two fighters closed in from astern, Jakobi on a level with the Fortress and Steinicke slightly below, the bomber's ventral gunner opened up. The Bf 109s returned fire, Jakobi scoring cannon hits on the starboard side of the Boeing's rear fuselage;

'The enemy was fishtailing in order to give his aft (i.e. *beam*) gunners a good field of fire. Because of my excess of speed, I came up alongside the enemy aircraft and could see a large hole in the rear third of the fuselage as well as flames coming from the upper part of the rudder.'

As Jakobi peeled away for another pass smoke began to pour from the bomber's port outer engine. Soon he was on its tail again. After banking slightly to the left, the Fortress jettisoned its load of six to eight bombs. The enemy gunners kept up a steady defensive fire as Jakobi bored in for a second attack. This time he saw his cannon shells strike home on the port wing. Large areas of the wing surface flew off.

Smoke was now billowing from the cockpit area too, and the Fortress began to spiral downwards. Jakobi shouted a warning to Steinicke, who was following it down, to get clear as it could blow up at any moment;

'The enemy aircraft went into a vertical dive and did then actually explode about 2000 m (6500 ft) below me. Blinded by the flash, I did not see the final impact.'

The wreckage in fact fell to earth in mountainous terrain near Bygland, some 75 km (46 miles) north of Kristiansand. Shortly afterwards Unteroffizier Karl-Heinz Woite brought down a second Fortress over the North Sea. The pair's success caused quite a stir in official circles, and on 17 September the following message was received from Generalleutnant Wilhelm Harmjanz, GOC *Luftgau Norwegen;*

'On 8.9.1941 Leutnant Jakobi and Unteroffizier Woite each shot down a Boeing, 75 km north of Kristiansund and 50 km south-west of Stavanger respectively. Please convey to those named my appreciation and heartiest congratulations.'

Technical experts from the RLM arrived in Norway to quiz Jakobi on details of the Boeing's defences, and were then taken to the crash site to investigate the wreckage. 'We've been dragged on wild goose chases from north to south and from east to west', Jakobi was told by them, 'and this is undoubtedly the first Flying Fortress to be shot down.'

The Boeing had been Jakobi's third kill. He would score seven victories before himself being hit and forced to bail out behind Russian lines on 9 April 1942, subsequently enduring many years of Soviet captivity until repatriation after the war.

The Bf 109T's operational career lasted a good two years longer than Jakobi's, the type remaining in frontline service over the North Sea region well into 1944, latterly with the *Jagdstaffel Helgoland* (11./JG 11). Surviving examples then saw out their days in training establishments.

This was in stark contrast to Jakobi's victim. 'D-Dog's' service life with No 90 Sqn had spanned a scant three weeks. But her demise at the end of that brief period has assured her of a toehold in aviation history as the very first of nearly 5000 Flying Fortresses to be lost in battle during World War 2.

COLOUR PLATES

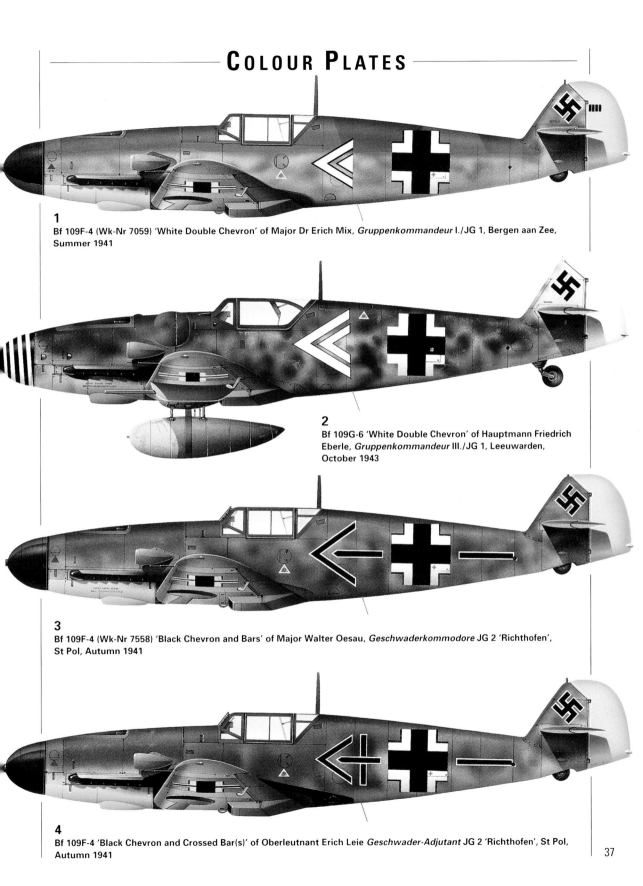

1
Bf 109F-4 (Wk-Nr 7059) 'White Double Chevron' of Major Dr Erich Mix, *Gruppenkommandeur* I./JG 1, Bergen aan Zee, Summer 1941

2
Bf 109G-6 'White Double Chevron' of Hauptmann Friedrich Eberle, *Gruppenkommandeur* III./JG 1, Leeuwarden, October 1943

3
Bf 109F-4 (Wk-Nr 7558) 'Black Chevron and Bars' of Major Walter Oesau, *Geschwaderkommodore* JG 2 'Richthofen', St Pol, Autumn 1941

4
Bf 109F-4 'Black Chevron and Crossed Bar(s)' of Oberleutnant Erich Leie *Geschwader-Adjutant* JG 2 'Richthofen', St Pol, Autumn 1941

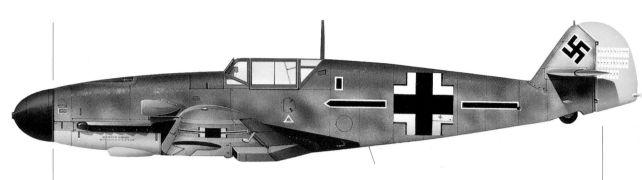

5
Bf 109F-4 'Black Bars and Dot' of Oberleutnant Rudolf Pflanz, *Geschwader-TO,* JG 2 'Richthofen', St Pol, Autumn 1941

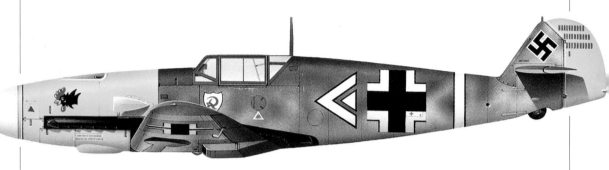

6
Bf 109F-2 (Wk-Nr 5749) 'White Double Chevron' of Hauptmann Hans Hahn, *Gruppenkommandeur* III./ JG 2 'Richthofen', St Pol, Summer 1941

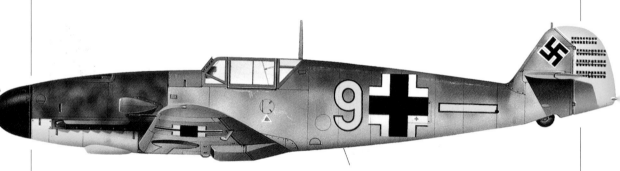

7
Bf 109F-4 (Wk-Nr 7650) 'Yellow 9' of Oberleutnant Erich Rudorffer, *Staffelkapitän* 6./JG 2 'Richthofen', Abbeville, Winter 1941-42

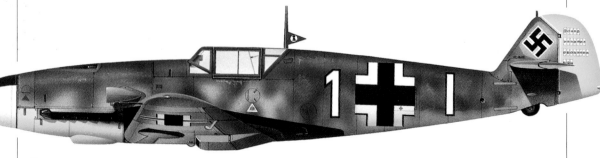

8
Bf 109F-2 (Wk-Nr 6720) 'White 1' of Oberleutnant Egon Mayer, *Staffelkapitän* 7./JG 2 'Richthofen', St Pol, Summer 1941

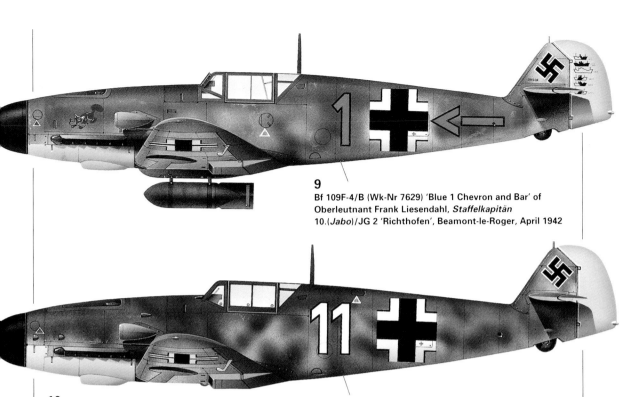

9
Bf 109F-4/B (Wk-Nr 7629) 'Blue 1 Chevron and Bar' of
Oberleutnant Frank Liesendahl, *Staffelkapitän*
10.(*Jabo*)/JG 2 'Richthofen', Beamont-le-Roger, April 1942

10
Bf 109G-1 (Wk-Nr 14063) 'White 11' of Oberleutnant Julius Meimberg, *Staffelkapitän* 11./JG 2 'Richthofen', Poix,
Summer 1942

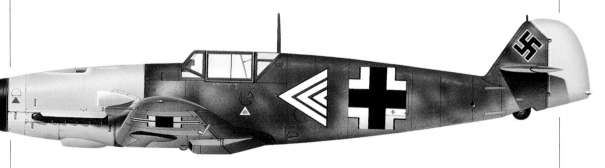

11
Bf 109F-2 (Wk-Nr 8117) 'White Triple Chevron' of Major Günther Lützow, *Geschwaderkommodore* JG 3,
Auchy-au-Bois, May 1941

12
Bf 109G-10/AS 'Black Double Chevron' of Oberleutnant Alfred Seidl, *Gruppenkommandeur* I./JG 3 'Udet', Paderborn,
December 1944

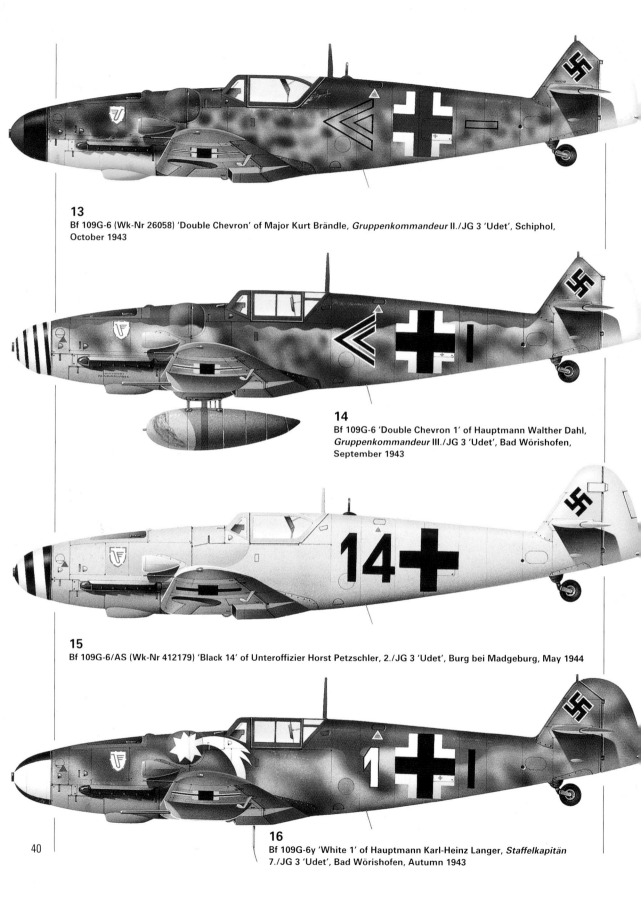

13
Bf 109G-6 (Wk-Nr 26058) 'Double Chevron' of Major Kurt Brändle, *Gruppenkommandeur* II./JG 3 'Udet', Schiphol, October 1943

14
Bf 109G-6 'Double Chevron 1' of Hauptmann Walther Dahl, *Gruppenkommandeur* III./JG 3 'Udet', Bad Wörishofen, September 1943

15
Bf 109G-6/AS (Wk-Nr 412179) 'Black 14' of Unteroffizier Horst Petzschler, 2./JG 3 'Udet', Burg bei Madgeburg, May 1944

16
Bf 109G-6y 'White 1' of Hauptmann Karl-Heinz Langer, *Staffelkapitän* 7./JG 3 'Udet', Bad Wörishofen, Autumn 1943

17
Bf 109G-14/ASy 'Black 13' of Oberleutnant Ernst Scheufele, *Staffelkapitän* 14./JG 4, Reinersdorf, October 1944

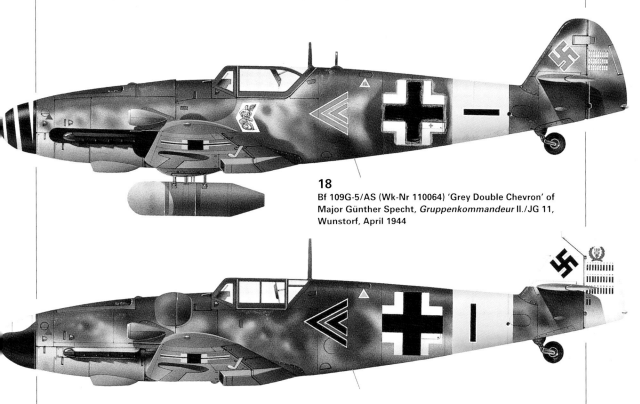

18
Bf 109G-5/AS (Wk-Nr 110064) 'Grey Double Chevron' of Major Günther Specht, *Gruppenkommandeur* II./JG 11, Wunstorf, April 1944

19
Bf 109G-6 'Black Double Chevron' of Hauptmann Anton Hackl, *Gruppenkommandeur* III./JG 11, Oldenburg, January 1944

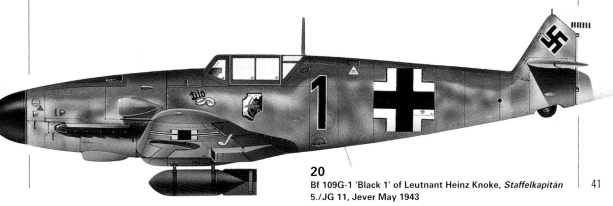

20
Bf 109G-1 'Black 1' of Leutnant Heinz Knoke, *Staffelkapitän* 5./JG 11, Jever May 1943

21
Bf 109T (Wk-Nr 7767) 'Black 6' of Oberleutnant Herbert Christmann, *Staffelkapitän* 11./JG 11, Lister/Norway, Spring 1944

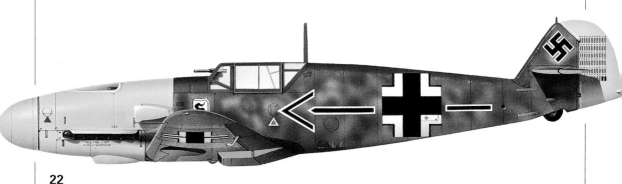

22
Bf 109F-2 (Wk-Nr 6714) 'Black Chevron and Bars' of Oberstleutnant Adolf Galland, *Geschwaderkommodore* JG 26 'Schlageter', Brest-Guipavas, April 1941

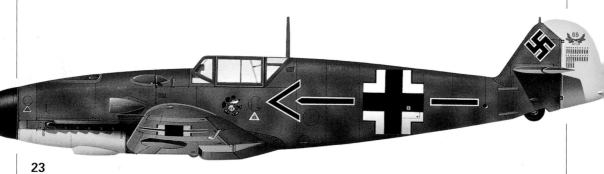

23
Bf 109F-2/U 'Black Chevron and Bars' of Oberstleutnant Adolf Galland, *Geschwaderkommodore* JG 26 'Schlageter', Audembert, November 1941

24
Bf 109F-2 'Black Double Chevron' of Hauptmann Gerhard Schöpfel, *Gruppenkommandeur* III./JG 26 'Schlageter', Liegescourt, Summer 1941

25
Bf 109G-6 'Black 22' of Major Klaus Mietusch,
Gruppenkommandeur III./JG 26 'Schlageter', Lille-Nord,
Spring 1944

26
Bf 109F-2 'Black 13' of Oberleutnant Gustav Sprick, *Staffelkapitän* 8./JG 26 'Schlageter', Liegescourt, June 1941

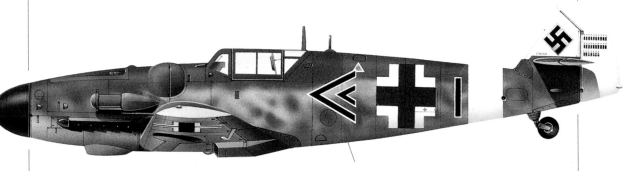

27
Bf 109G-6 trop (Wk-Nr 140139) 'Black Double Chevron' of Major Ernst Düllberg, *Gruppenkommandeur* III./JG 27,
Wiesbaden-Erbenheim, March 1944

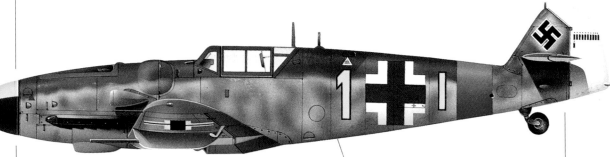

28
Bf 109G-6 'Yellow 1'' of Leutnant Dr Peter Werfft, *Staffelkapitän* 9./JG 27, Vienna-Seyring, March 1944

29
Bf 109G-6 (Wk-Nr 15913) 'Red 1' of Major Hermann Graf, *Gruppenkommandeur* JG(r) 50, Wiesbaden-Erbenheim,
September 1943

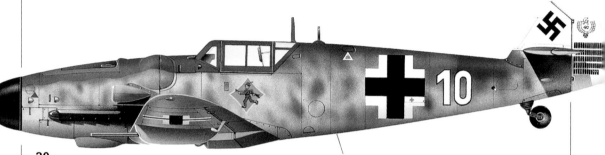

30
Bf 109G-6 'White 10' of Oberleutnant Alfred Grislawski, *Staffelkapitän* of 1./JG 50, Wiesbaden-Erbenheim,
September 1943

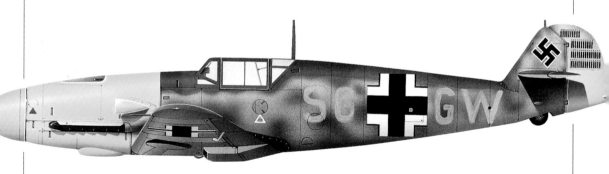

31
Bf 109F-1 (Wk-Nr 5628) of Major Werner Mölders, *Geschwaderkommodore* JG 51, St Omer, November 1940

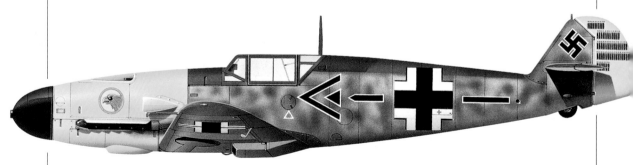

32
Bf 109F-1 'Black Double Chevron and Bars' of Major Werner Mölders, *Geschwaderkommodore* JG 51, Mardyck, April 1941

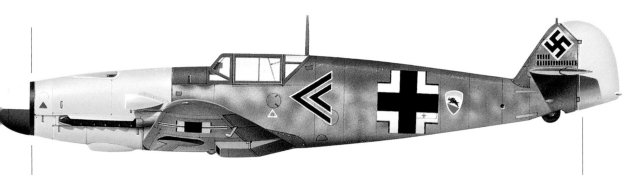

33
Bf 109F-2 (Wk-Nr 8155) 'Black Double Chevron' of Hauptmann Karl-Heinz Leesmann, *Gruppenkommandeur* I./JG 52, Leeuwarden, Summer 1941

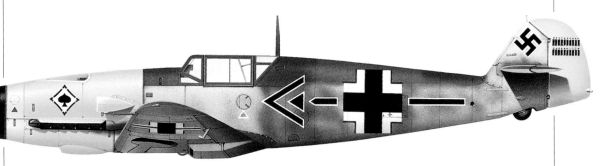

34
Bf 109F-2 (Wk-Nr 6683) 'Black Chevron and Bars' of Major Günther von Maltzahn, *Geschwaderkommodore* JG 53 '*Pik-As*', St Omer-Wizernes, May 1941

35
Bf 109F-2 (Wk-Nr 6674) 'Black Double Chevron' of Hauptmann Heinz Bretnütz, *Gruppenkommandeur* of II./JG 53 '*Pik-As*', St Omer-Clairmarais, May 1941

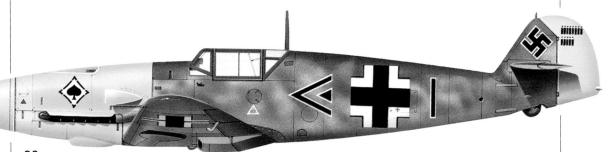

36
Bf 109F-2 'Black Double Chevron' of Hauptmann Wolf-Dietrich Wilcke, *Gruppenkommandeur* III./JG 53 '*Pik-As*', Berck-sur-Mer, May 1941

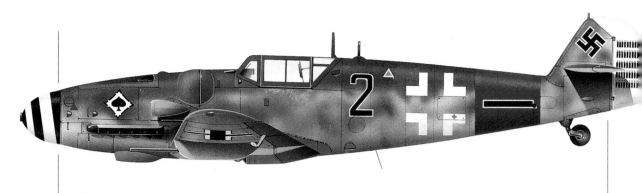

37
Bf 109G-6 'Black 2' of Oberfeldwebel Herbert Rollwage, 5./JG 53 *'Pik-As'*, Vienna-Seyring, January 1944

38
Bf 109K-4 'Yellow 1' of Leutnant Günther Landt, *Staffelkapitän* 11./JG 53 *'Pik-As'*, Kirrlach, February 1945

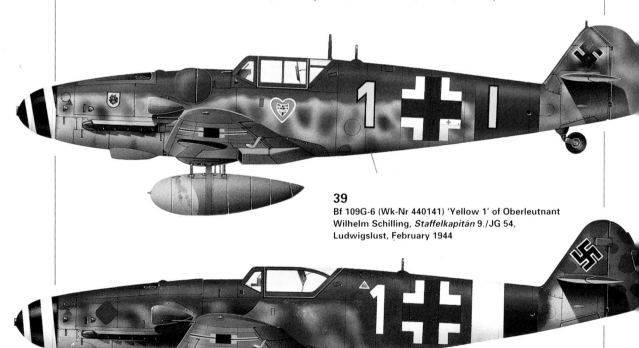

39
Bf 109G-6 (Wk-Nr 440141) 'Yellow 1' of Oberleutnant Wilhelm Schilling, *Staffelkapitän* 9./JG 54, Ludwigslust, February 1944

40
Bf 109K-4 (Wk-Nr 330204) 'White 1' of Hauptmann Menzel, *Staffelkapitän* 9./JG 77, Neuruppin, December 1944

DEFENCE OF THE REICH

In the opening weeks of 1943 the daylight air war in the west entered a new phase which would lock the *Jagdwaffe* into an irrevocably defensive posture. In retrospect, the previous years of cross-Channel sparring, where individual opponents had become almost familiar, if not by name, then by mannerism – 'the flyer in the white silk scarf', or 'the pilot who always flew No 13' – would appear positively chivalrous. Henceforth, the scale of operations would occupy an ever broader canvas as the full weight of US air power was brought to bear on Nazi Germany itself until, ultimately, huge aerial armadas of American bombers, and their escorting fighters, were parading almost at will into the furthermost recesses of the Führer's Reich.

And while it might be an exaggeration to describe the Luftwaffe's response to these assaults in terms of 'armadas', entire *Gruppen* or even *Geschwader* of defending fighters would – initially, at least – be sent up to do battle where previously single *Schwärme* or *Staffeln* had sufficed.

The first US daylight heavy bomber raid on a target inside Germany's borders was that launched on 27 January 1943 by 50+ B-17s against Wilhelmshaven naval base (the same objective, incidentally, as had been assigned to the Wellingtons involved in the 'Battle of the German Bight' three years earlier). This time the opposition was provided by Hauptmann Günther Beise's I./JG 1. Although the *Gruppe* claimed five kills, only one Fortress was, in fact, shot down. Against this, five Bf 109G-1s were lost, with three pilots killed.

It was not an altogether auspicious start, and seemed only to confirm official thinking (reinforced by the successes already achieved by the two Channel-based *Jagdgeschwader*) that the Fw 190 was by far the more formidable bomber-killer.

Nevertheless when, almost exactly a month later, on 26 February, the Eighth AF again struck at Wilhelmshaven, Beise's *Gustavs* were credited with eight of the thirteen 'heavies' claimed. Among the victors that day was Oberleutnant Hugo Frey, *Staffelkapitän* of 2./JG 1, whose B-24 took his score to five. Frey would emerge high on the list of *Jagdwaffe* pilots who were successful against four-engined bombers, 26 of his final total of 32 being 'heavies', including the last four brought down on 6 March 1944 during the US raid on Berlin which also cost his own life.

Another 2. *Staffel* pilot to claim a B-24 on that 26 February had been Heinz Knoke. It was his third kill. Two more 'heavies' in March would make Knoke I. *Gruppe's* second ace, and like Frey, he too would become an undisputed *Viermot-Experte*, with 19 four-engined bombers numbered among his final of 33. Unlike Frey, however, all Knoke's victories were achieved on the Bf 109 – *and* he survived the war, although he never flew on operations again after being severely wounded by partisan action during a transfer by road in October 1944.

With the Eighth AF now beginning to strike at targets within Germany proper, moves were made in February 1943 to increase the Reich's day-light aerial defences. At this time these were controlled by I. *Jagdkorps*, some three-quarters of whose 400+ serviceable aircraft were made up of nightfighters – the remaining 100 were single-seaters of JG 1's four *Gruppen*. It was a sign of the changing priorities of the air war, and of just how thinly stretched the *Jagdwaffe* was becoming, that *Gruppen* were now to be stripped from other theatres, who could ill afford to lose them, to bolster fighter strength in the homeland and western Europe.

All three of the new arrivals in the west early in 1943 were *Gruppen* equipped with the Bf 109. Strictly speaking, the first of these constituted a replacement rather than reinforcement. One of *General der Jagdflieger* Galland's more ill-conceived schemes was the exchange of an entire eastern front *Jagdgeschwader* with one from the Channel front. Just what advantages would derive from this (apart from providing those involved with a change of scenery), and whether these would outweigh the inevitable disruption caused, and dangers posed, by the unavoidable period of acclimatisation each would have to undergo in its new environment, was not made clear.

Common sense prevailed in the end, however, and only one *Gruppe* of each of the *Geschwader* selected actually made the switch. There was one difference. Whereas I./JG 26 and their Fw 190s returned to the west after some four months' absence in Russia, III./JG 54's departure from the Eastern front was to prove permanent.

Commanded by Major Reinhard 'Seppl' Seiler, III./JG 54 arrived at Vendeville in France on 12 February 1943. Operating at first on a semi-autonomous basis, the *Gruppe* moved to Oldenburg the following month to add their weight to the defences of Germany's North Sea coastal region. A wholly different kind of war awaited them there, and the flaws inherent in Galland's exchange scheme – which saw fit to pit low-level Eastern front *Experten* against high-flying American heavy bombers – quickly became all too apparent.

Among their long list of casualties were two Knight's Cross holders, who were both killed in action against B-17s near Heligoland on 15 May. Each had at least 50 Soviet kills to his credit. But it is believed that Hauptmann Günther Fink, *Staffelkapitän* of 8./JG 54, had not scored once since arriving in the west over three months earlier, and that 7. *Staffel's* Leutnant Friedrich Rupp had gained just two kills (admittedly both four-engined bombers) in the same period.

After a brief deployment in the Low Countries, III./JG 54 was transferred to the Hamburg area in the late summer of 1943. Here, it continued to suffer losses for little return, until finally being withdrawn from frontline service in April 1944 for re-equipment with the Fw 190.

The second newcomer to France in the early weeks of 1943 had at least had recent operational experience against the western Allies, albeit over North Africa. The departure of JG 27 from the Libyan desert – a theatre of war with which it is indissolubly linked – marked the end of a chapter in the unit's history. After rest and re-equipment, the bulk of the *Geschwader* continued to serve in the Mediterranean. I. *Gruppe*, however, having exchanged its desert-weary *Friedrichs* for new Bf 109G-4s, was to take up station in France alongside JG 2.

By this time I./JG 27 bore little relation to its former self. Many of its pilots were fresh from training school, and it had a brand new *Kommandeur* straight from the Eastern front. Its fortunes were mixed. While some of the old hands quickly settled in – Oberleutnant Karl von Lieres und Wilkau, *Staffelkapitän* of 3./JG 27, claimed an American B-17 north of Saint-Lô on 8 March and a British Mosquito 24 hours later – others were finding it more difficult.

Gruppenkommandeur Heinrich Setz, winner of the Oak Leaves with a tally of 132 Soviet aircraft to his credit, was an early casualty. On 13 March the entire *Gruppe* was scrambled to intercept an incoming formation of B-17s. Setz led his *Stabsschwarm* up towards the Spitfire escort, and in the ensuing melée high above Abbeville, he claimed no fewer than three of the enemy fighters. But then his own machine was seen to plummet almost vertically to the ground far below. Whether Setz had fallen victim to another Spitfire, or had collided with a fourth opponent, was never positively established.

Having transferred in the meantime from Bernay to Poix, and commanded now by Hauptmann Erich Hohagen, a Knight's Cross veteran of JG 2, I./JG 27 also enjoyed early success near Abbeville when it bounced a squadron of RAF Typhoons on 18 April and reportedly brought down seven of them. The following month it was 2. *Staffel's* turn. On detachment to JG 1 at Leeuwarden, in Holland, Hauptmann Ernst Maak's 2./JG 27 were credited with five of the 24 B-17s claimed by the defending fighters on 21 May (although, in reality, US losses were exactly half that number).

On 1 June 1943 Erich Hohagen was severely wounded in one of the *Gruppe's* last engagements over north-west Europe, and shortly thereafter I./JG 27 was transferred to the south of France. But they would soon return to Defence of the Reich duties. And they would later be joined by the other *Gruppen* of the *Geschwader*. Fully reunited, JG 27's Bf 109s would then play an integral, and valuable, part in the closing stages of the desperate struggle to protect the Homeland.

The last of the initial trio of *Gruppen* to be added to the western

As well as the *Afrika* badge seen on the brand new Bf 109G-4 parked in the background, I./JG 27 brought back to Europe another, more tangible, reminder of their days in the desert – prisoner of war Matthew Letuku, an ex-corporal in the South African army who had served as Hans-Joachim Marseille's driver and batman! By now an accepted member of the *Gruppe*, 'Mathias' remained with them until mid-1944 (and was a surprise guest at a JG 27 reunion forty years later!)

49

When armed with an additional pair of MG 151/20 cannon in underwing gondolas, as carried by this G-6 pictured in northern France in the summer of 1943, the *Gustav* was a potent 'bomber-killer'

defences could not have come from a more different background than I./JG 27. While the latter's previous environs had been the sandy, burning wastes of North Africa, Hauptmann Klaus Quaet-Faslem's I./JG 3 had been operating over the equally featureless tracts of the Russian steppe in mid-winter as they supported the 6. *Armee's* advance on Stalingrad. Their final actions in the east had been fought over the besieged city in mid-January 1943.

In contrast to the original I./JG 3, which had been redesignated II./JG 1 shortly after its transfer from east to west a year earlier, Quaet-Faslem's *Gruppe* would retain their identity. Like I./JG 27 before them, they too represented but the first step of their parent *Geschwader's* subsequent transition in its entirety into a Reich's Defence *Geschwader*.

Although the *Gruppe's* swingeing losses at Stalingrad had been made good with a full complement of new Bf 109G-4s by the time of their arrival at München-Gladbach in April 1943, I./JG 3 did not commence operations until June. By then they were taking delivery of their first G-6 *Kanonenboote* (gunboats). These had the *Gustav's* single engine-mounted cannon augmented by a pair of similar guns in underwing gondolas. Thus equipped, I./JG 3 was deemed a fully-fledged 'bomber-killer' *Gruppe*.

Their relatively lengthy period of working-up appears to have paid off, for the *Gruppe* was soon taking a steady toll of American B-17s without suffering the concomitant heavy losses in return. Among the claimants was Quaet-Faslem himself, whose first two Fortresses – brought down exactly a month apart, on 17 July and 17 August respectively – took his total score to 48. Two other Eastern front *Experten*, both already Knight's Cross holders, claimed their first 'heavies' during these same two months. Oberleutnant Helmut Mertens, *Staffelkapitän* of 1./JG 3, got two B-17s, raising his tally to 53, while the single Fortress downed on 19 August by 2. *Staffel's* recently commissioned Leutnant Franz Schwaiger was his 56th kill, confirming his position as the *Gruppe's* current top scorer.

But even before I./JG 3 had been declared operational, the Luftwaffe High Command had devised another method of strengthening their aerial defences in the west. Just as the rapid expansion programmes of the prewar years had relied heavily on individual units being split to provide cadres for one or more new formations – the so-called 'mother' and 'daughter' system – so now JG 1 would be divided to create a whole new *Geschwader*.

On 1 April 1943 two of JG 1's four *Gruppen* were redesignated to become part of this new unit. One of the two was Günther Beise's Bf 109-equipped I./JG 1, which would henceforth operate as II./JG 11. Each *Geschwader* was also required to activate a fresh III. *Gruppe* from scratch. The new III./JG 1, under Major Karl-Heinz Leesmann, immediately received a full complement of Bf 109G-6s, whilst III./JG 11 apparently had to wait a little longer for their *Gustavs*, which they would then begin to exchange for Fw 190s by year's end.

Just as JG 1 had split, amoeba-like, into two, so the *Geschwader's* areas of responsibility – which had previously encompassed both the Dutch and German North Sea coastal belts – were now also clearly separated and delineated . . . at least on the staffers' maps. The reconstituted JG 1 took up residence in the Netherlands, leaving the 'new' JG 11 to protect the German Bight.

Thus, by mid-1943 Bf 109 strength in the west was concentrated in eight main *Gruppen*. Five of these were deployed along the Channel and North Sea coastlines, from the Biscay to the German Bight, in company with the Fw 190 units of their parent *Geschwader*. From west to east these five *Gruppen* were II./JG 2, III./JG 26, III./JG 1 and II. and III./JG 11. The first two, as their surviving members still take pains to point out, formed part of *Luftflotte* 3, the 'frontline' Air Fleet guarding the outermost ramparts of occupied north-western Europe against all comers.

The as yet still semi-autonomous I./JG 27 also came under *Luftflotte* 3's control for much of this period, as too did III./JG 54 for a short while. The three Bf 109 *Gruppen* of JGs 1 and 11, on the other hand, together with I./JG 3, were subordinated to *Luftwaffenbefehlshaber Mitte* (the forerunner of *Luftflotte Reich*) purely in defence of the Homeland.

The summer of 1943 was still very much a time of expansion for the Eighth AF. The American bombers had not yet attained the overwhelming superiority in numbers which would ultimately swamp the defending

... but it's business as usual for III./JG 26. Here a *Rotte* of 9. *Staffel* G-6s prepares to take off from Wevelghem in the late spring of 1943

An experienced pilot discourses on the art of bringing down a heavy bomber. He appears to be advocating the head-on attack. Judging from their expressions, his listeners – especially the one on his immediate right – are far from convinced

In the hand of an *Experte* the G-6 *'Kanonenboot'* was more than a match for a heavy bomber. Cheering pilots – one enthusiastically waving his own 'victory stick' – greet a friend's return from an obviously successful sortie

Jagdwaffe. More importantly, they still lacked long-range fighter escort. The outcome of the daylight battle for the Reich was, at this stage, by no means decided. The *Jagdgruppen*, quick to learn from experience to bide their time until the escorting fighters were forced to break off due to lack of fuel, inflicted some heavy losses on the enemy during the latter half of the year as the bombers began to venture deeper into Reich airspace.

Sitting astride the 'heavies'' main routes of approach into north-western Germany, JGs 1 and 11 bore the brunt of much of the action. Indeed, their six component *Gruppen* were responsible for over 40 per cent of the 1200+ claims submitted in the area during these months. The earlier official pedantry which directed the Bf 109 units towards whatever fighter escort was in attendance, leaving the Fw 190s to concentrate on the

bomber boxes, became an irrelevance in the heat and confusion of the running battles now being fought. All three Bf 109 *Gruppen* began to add a steady quota of heavy bombers (mainly B-17s) to their scoreboards.

JG 11's EXPERTEN

Not surprisingly, perhaps, some of the most successful pilots came from the ranks of the 'veteran' II./JG 11 (ex-I./JG 1). Two *Staffelkapitäne*, in particular, had added significantly to their scores before the year was out. Hauptmann Gerhard Sommer of 4./JG 11 increased his total from three to 17, with ten of his victims' being four-engined 'heavies'. 5. *Staffel's* Oberleutnant Heinz Knoke likewise claimed 14 kills (including 12 heavy bombers) during the same period.

5./JG 11, in fact, regarded themselves as the Gruppe's *Viermot-Experten*, and with some justification, for they were credited with as many four-engined bombers as the other two *Staffeln* put together. Among the methods they used was the frontal attack, developed and already being practised to great effect by the Channel-based *Jagdgeschwader*. They also employed underwing rockets, which were fired from a distance to break up the bombers' carefully structured combat boxes. But undoubtedly their most novel way of dealing with the bombers was to bomb them!

The idea of slinging a bomb beneath a Bf 109 and then dropping it on a close-packed formation of US 'heavies' from above had first been proposed by a friend of Knoke's, Leutnant Dieter Gerhardt, when the two were serving together in 2./JG 1. The latter pilot was killed in action against B-24s on 18 March 1943, but Knoke persisted with the experiments the pair had begun.

Four days after Gerhardt's loss, Knoke put his theory to the ultimate test. With a 250-kg bomb under the belly of his *Gustav*, he climbed towards a formation of B-17s which had just attacked Wilhelmshaven. High above Heligoland, he slid into position over the leading Fortress of the box. Despite the fire from below – he would later find eight holes in his Messerschmitt – Knoke took rough and ready aim, dipping first one wing and then the other to keep the enemy formation in sight, and to be able to judge his height and distance from the target.

After releasing his bomb Knoke climbed higher still, banking to watch over his shoulder as the missile fell. It detonated in the middle of a vic of three bombers. The wing of one was immediately sheared off, whilst the other two dived steeply away in alarm. The B-17 plunged into the North Sea some 30 km (18 miles) west of Heligoland. The severed wing followed it down, 'fluttering like an autumn leaf'.

The effect of, and circumstances behind, Knoke's fifth kill (his third heavy bomber) reverberated upwards throughout the Luftwaffe chain of command until it reached the very top. That night the lowly Leutnant – famously minus his pyjama bottoms, for Knoke's preferred night attire was just the jacket – was woken from his slumbers by a congratulatory telephone call from *Reichsmarschall* Hermann Göring himself: 'I am pleased by the initiative you have shown and wish to express my appreciation in person'. As Knoke said later: 'If Hermann had only known that I didn't even have any trousers on!'

Since promoted to the command of 5./JG 11, and now with official blessing, Knoke continued his air-to-air bombing experiments. 5. *Staffel* achieved a string of successes using the new technique. These culminated in the action of 28 July when 5./JG 11's bomb-laden *Gustavs* were responsible for no fewer than seven of the 12 B-17s credited to their parent *Gruppe*. Undisputed hero of that 'Day of the great shooting party' (5. *Staffel* had initially claimed 11 bombers downed) was Unteroffizier Wilhelm Fest, who destroyed three Fortresses with a single bomb.

Strangely, the Americans appear to have been completely unaware of the bombing attack to which they had been subjected. They attributed the loss of Fest's three victims to a rocket strike. But 5./JG 11 reportedly did not begin using underwing rockets until the following month, by which time the *Staffel's* unique 'bombing campaign' had run its course. The growing threat posed by US escort fighters made the skies of western Germany a perilous place for bomb-carrying Messerschmitts. From now on the *Jagdwaffe* would rely on underwing rockets and cannon as their main instruments of bomber destruction.

One who used these more conventional weapons with undoubted success was II./JG 11's new *Gruppenkommandeur*. Assuming command early in May, Hauptmann Günther Specht was an ex-*Zerstörer* pilot (see *Osprey Aircraft of the Aces 25 - Messerschmitt Bf 110 Zerstörer Aces of World War 2* for further details) who had lost an eye in action in the early months of the war. Despite this disability, the diminutive Specht was still an excellent marksman. By the end of the year he had added a further 17 victories to his tally, taking his total to 24, and making him the *Gruppe's* then highest scorer.

Seemingly far outstripping Specht at the close of 1943 was fellow *Gruppenkommandeur* Major Anton Hackl with 130 enemy aircraft to his credit. But Hackl had only taken over III./JG 11 in October. Prior to that he had been a long-time member of II./JG 77, with service in both Russia and the Mediterranean (he was badly wounded in Tunisia in February 1943). Hackl downed 'only' four or five heavy bombers while leading III./JG 11 before the *Gruppe* converted to Fw 190s. He was one of the exceptions which proved the rule – an ex-Eastern front pilot who became arguably even more successful in the west (perhaps the interlude in North Africa aided the transition).

The other main weapon in the *Gustav's* anti-bomber armoury was the 210 mm air-to-air rocket. These unidentified early Reich's defence G-6s, with rockets already loaded in their underwing launch tubes, await the 'heavies'' approach

Hackl was well known for keeping two aircraft on standby: a Bf 109 which he would fly if his opponents were likely to be fighters, and a Fw 190 if he were going up against heavy bombers. The latter obviously saw its fair share of use, for he ended the war as the third-ranking bomber-killer with 32 'heavies' numbered among his overall total of 192.

The unfortunate Major Karl-Heinz Leesmann ran truer to form. He had been in command of I./JG 52 during the early stages of the campaign in the east, but had been very seriously wounded in November 1941. Long classed as unfit for flying duties, he was finally appointed *Gruppenkommandeur* of the new III./JG 1 upon its activation in April 1943. It obviously took him some while to find his feet, for he did not claim his first kill – a B-17 – until 25 June. He then downed a brace of Beaufighters attacking a convoy off the Dutch coast on 18 July, followed by another Fortress exactly a week later (these four victories – some sources credit him with five – made Leesmann the *Gruppe's* top scorer, which is quite a reflection on III./JG 1's kill rate during this hectic summer of 1943).

Return fire from his final victim on 25 July 1943 mortally damaged Leesmann's *Gustav*, however, and it too disappeared into the North Sea. III./JG 1 would earn something of a reputation as a 'hard luck' outfit, for not only had they lost their first *Kommandeur*, but five *Staffelkapitäne* would also be killed before the year was out.

SPECIAL *GRUPPE*

Among a number of smaller formations operating the Bf 109 over the Reich in mid-1943 was the so-called JG 50. In reality, this was a special unit of single *Gruppe* strength, and hence often referred to as JGr 50, which had been activated at Wiesbaden-Erbenheim for the express purpose of combating high-flying American bombers and RAF reconnaissance intruders. Command of JG 50 was given to one of the most successful of all Eastern front *Experten*, wearer of the Oak Leaves with Swords and Diamonds, and the first Luftwaffe fighter pilot to reach the double 'century' – Major Hermann Graf.

Graf brought down at least two B-17s (on 6 September) while leading JG 50. And when that unit was disbanded in November he was appointed *Kommodore* of JG 11. Over the next four months he would be credited with another half-dozen American aircraft destroyed, including three P-51s. The last two were claimed north of Hannover on 29 March 1944, the first of which he shot down, and the second he rammed – whether unintentionally or by design is not clear. Either way, he himself was badly injured and had to take to his parachute. After recovering from his wounds, he would return to the Eastern front and JG 52.

As the late summer of 1943 gave way to early autumn, the Luftwaffe High Command, fully aware of the fact that their home-based fighters were hurting the Eighth AF, notched up the pressure by introducing a second wave of reinforcements to their Reich's Defence organisation. The main aim of this present expansion was to provide another complete *Jagdgeschwader* to protect Germany's western borders. To this end II. and III./JG 3 were pulled out of Russia, where they had been deployed on the southern flank of the failed Kursk salient offensive, and returned to the Homeland to join I./JG 3 and the *Geschwaderstab* early in August.

Major Hermann Graf, Eastern front ace and the first pilot in the world to achieve the double 'century', also commanded JGs 50, 1 and 11 in Defence of the Reich, where he was credited with ten victories

Not far behind Graf came the lesser
known Joachim Kirschner, whose
final score of 188 included 21
claimed over the Mediterranean and
in the west. Seated on his G-6,
Oberleutnant Kirschner is pictured
here in the late summer of 1943
when he was the *Staffelkapitän* of
5./JG 3 'Udet'. Note the large red
dot immediately below the 'Winged
U' *Geschwader* badge . . .

In line with persisting doctrine, which still stipulated that home-
defence *Geschwader* should consist of two anti-bomber *Gruppen* and one
Gruppe of covering fighters, Major Kurt Brändle's II./JG 3 received a
batch of high-altitude Bf 109G-5s to add to the G-6s with which they had
begun re-equipping just before leaving the Eastern front. They were now
classed as the *Geschwader's 'leichte'* ('light') *Gruppe*, and officially tasked
with protecting the other two. The reality of combat would dictate otherwise, for in the closing months of 1943 they would down as many, if not
more, heavy bombers than enemy fighters.

This left III./JG 3, under Hauptmann Walther Dahl, to shoulder the

. . . which is also visible in this shot
of two pilots lighting up – in
dangerous proximity to that
bandoleer of signal cartridges! –
alongside another of II./JG 3's
Gustavs. Although its exact
significance is not known, the dot
below the *Geschwader* badge was a
common feature on the *Gruppe's*
aircraft at this period

Walther Dahl, *Gruppenkommandeur* of III./JG 3 'Udet', is pictured being strapped into the cockpit of a G-6 which still retains the two small fairings below the windscreen (used to affix a sun umbrella) more commonly associated with tropicalised machines

G-6y *'Kanonenboot'* 'Yellow 6' of 9./JG 3 is seen at Bad Wörishofen in September 1943. Sitting on the port mainwheel is pilot Oberfeldwebel Alfred Surau, who would add five B-17s to the 41 victories he had claimed in the east before he himself was wounded and forced to bail out of this machine during the USAF's second Schweinfurt raid of 14 October (he died of his wounds later the same day). Note 9. *Staffel's* elaborate 'eye' painted on the bulge ahead of the cockpit

'bomber-killer' role. For this they were initially equipped, like I./JG 3 before them, with G-6 *Kanonen-boote* armed with underwing cannon – rocket launchers were also later added to their armoury.

Having been accustomed to flying mainly low-level *freie Jagd*-type sweeps in *Schwarm*, or at most *Staffel*, strength in the east, both *Gruppen* were subjected to an intensive working-up programme which was designed to prepare them for their new theatre of operations. Although undoubtedly helpful, this period of acclimatisation – the calm before the storm – would be all too brief.

II. and III./JG 3 were not the only new additions to the Reich's aerial defences at this juncture. At the same time two other *Gruppen* arrived from the south. II./JG 27 and II./JG 51 had both been withdrawn from Italy, thereby further denuding what was already being referred to as the 'soft underbelly of Europe'. But while the transfer would prove permanent for Hauptmann Werner Schroer's II./JG 27, Major Karl Rammelt and his II./JG 51 remained only a matter of weeks in the Homeland. They would find themselves back in Italy by year's end, before then being moved across into the Balkans.

This latest strengthening of Germany's defences coincided with an all-out effort by the Eighth AF which was intended to prove beyond doubt the integrity of the American policy of daylight attack by formations of unescorted, heavily-armed bombers. On 17 August the entire weight of their UK-based B-17 bomber force – 16 groups totalling some 375

aircraft in all – was despatched against two vital industrial targets deep inside Germany: the aircraft factories at Regensburg and the ball-bearing plants at Schweinfurt. The result was a disaster – 60 B-17s missing and nearly three times that number damaged.

It is believed that elements of at least ten western- and Reich-based Bf 109 *Gruppen* took part in this epic aerial battle. Altogether, they claimed close on 50 B-17s destroyed (plus a handful of P-47 fighters during the opening and closing stages). Even taking into account the inevitable duplication arising out of *Herausschüsse* and *endgültige Vernichtungen*, these figures for the number of 'heavies' shot down are clearly exaggerated. The seven participating Fw 190 Gruppen, still the *Jagdwaffe's* 'official' bomber-killers, undoubtedly achieved more than ten victories between them (to say nothing of the twin-engined fighters and the heavy flak also encountered by the bombers).

Since the early days of the war, when the destruction of 20 enemy aircraft automatically qualified a pilot for the Knight's Cross, the Luftwaffe had introduced a strict points system as a yardstick for the conferring of awards and decorations. By these criteria the shooting down of an enemy fighter was worth one point, a twin-engined bomber two points and a four-engined bomber four points. Such were the complications often surrounding the demise of a heavy bomber, however, that two further categories of 'success' were recognised.

A *Herausschuss* (literally a 'shooting-out' or, in other words, a 'separation') was the term applied to the damaging of a heavy bomber to such an extent that it was forced to drop out of station and be deprived of the mutually protective fire of its combat box. A *Herausschuß* won the assailant two points. An *endgültige Vernichtung* ('final destruction') referred to the *coup de grâce* subsequently administered to any such separated and damaged straggler. This last act in the drama was worth one point. By the same token, the 'separation' and 'despatch' of twin-engined bombers – frequent opponents of those *Jagdgruppen* based nearer to the coast – were valued at one and a half-point respectively.

Among the first fighters to engage on 17 August 1943 were the *Gustavs* of III./JG 26, currently on detachment to Schiphol, in the Netherlands. Of the ten Fortresses they reportedly downed, two went to recently-appointed *Gruppenkommandeur* Hauptmann Klaus Meitusch, who had been a member of JG 26 since before the war. Another pair were claimed

9./JG 3's 'eye' was eclipsed by 7./JG 3's even more striking 'comet' emblem (see colour profile no 16) But, as far as is known, the other *Staffel* in the *Gruppe*, 8./JG 3, carried no such markings. This shot of an emergency scramble by III./JG 3's 'Alarmrotte' at Schiphol would seem to confirm this, for the 'Beulen' of the G-6s towards which the two pilots are sprinting are devoid of any decorations whatsoever

by Oberfeldwebel Heinz Kemethmüller, an experienced NCO pilot with the Knight's Cross and more than 70 kills already to his credit (the majority from previous service on the Eastern front).

Later in the action Hauptmann Hermann Staiger, *Staffelkapitän* of 12./JG 26, claimed a single B-17 – his sixth heavy bomber in the space of a month. Staiger would survive the war flying Me 262 jets with JG 7. Ranked fifth-equal among the *Viermot-Experten* (alongside Frey, Hermichen and Schroer), all but four of his 26 'heavies' came on the *Gustav.*

Given the discrepancies in postwar references (the most glaring of those, perhaps, being the mistyping, or misreading from an original document, of Herbert Rollwage's score of 'heavies' as 44 – which would make him far and away the most successful of all - whereas recent research has revealed the actual figure to be a more modest, but nonetheless creditable 14), Staiger may well have legitimate claim to be one of the highest-scoring Bf 109 pilots against four-engined bombers in the west. Only Werner Schroer is believed to have brought down more 'heavies' while flying the Bf 109, but nearly half of his successes were gained in the Mediterranean.

But whatever the merits, or otherwise, of such hind-sighted 'number crunching', III./JG 26's performance in the opening rounds of the Schweinfurt-Regensburg battle set a broad pattern for the *Gruppen* which followed. It was usually the experienced formation leaders who achieved the kills and the 'rank-and-filers' who fell victim to the bombers' defensive fire – though not to the tune of the 228 claimed by the latter! Of the four B-17s credited to II./JG 11, for example, two were downed by *Kommandeur* Hauptmann Günther Specht, and a third by *Staffelkapitän* Heinz Knoke.

Top scorers of all the *Gruppen* were the 'specialists' of JG 50, whose Wiesbaden base lay almost directly in the path of the embattled bombers' route to Regensburg. Reinforced by experienced instructors from nearby training establishments, JG 50 sent some 30 fighters up to attack the passing B-17s and claimed no fewer than 16 of them.

Knight's Cross holder Leutnant Alfred Grislawski had been a long-time member of Graf's 9./JG 52 in the east, and had accompanied his *Staffelkapitän* back to the Reich;

'As we climbed I got my first good look at an American formation. There were so many of them! It shook us all; our small group of *'Alte Hasen'* (lit. 'old hares', i.e. veterans) from Russia, as well as the youngsters.

With his 'anti-bomber' bombing campaign well and truly over, the ventral bomb rack was removed from Heinz Knoke's G-1 and underwing rocket tubes fitted instead. Points of interest on 'Black 1' are the *Gruppe* badge of II./JG 11, just visible below the cockpit sill, and the narrow red band around the aft fuselage. Keen eyes will also note the absence of the additional air scoop above the supercharger air intake which normally characterised the high-altitude G-1 (this was presumably due to a replacement cowling from a non-pressurised machine)

We split into *Schwärme* and launched a series of frontal attacks. A number of the young pilots broke away prematurely, obviously put off by the ferocity of the return fire.'

The savage mauling suffered by the Eighth AF during the Schweinfurt-Regensburg operation added further weight to the serious consideration already being given to operating the 'heavies' by night. In the event, nothing came of this. The B-17s and B-24s would continue to fly daylight missions, reliance being placed instead on a promised increase in numbers by new units arriving from the States. Unlike the *Jagdwaffe*, the Eighth AF did not have to resort to pilferage from other theatres to boost its strength. But when a return visit was made to Schweinfurt on 14 October 1943, it was the same 16 groups of B-17s which were involved. The results of this second strike were almost a re-run of the first, with another 60 bombers being lost (although the number of B-17s damaged was slightly down).

As a result of these unacceptably high casualties, no further deep penetration raids would be flown until suitable fighter cover could be provided. A start had already been made in this direction. On 27 September a force of over 300 B-17s had attacked Emden – admittedly a coastal target – and returned with the loss of only seven bombers. They had been escorted all the way to their objective and back by P-47s equipped, for the first time, with 108 US gallon drop tanks. But it would be the appearance of the P-51 Mustang at the close of the year which would herald the true beginning of the end for the Defence of the Reich *Jagdgruppen*.

For if the Schweinfurt raids had represented the nadir of the Eighth AF's fortunes (from which it would recover to grow even stronger), the same period can also be said to mark the pinnacle of the *Jagdwaffe*'s performance in the west, after which they, by contrast, would find

How many mechanics does it take to push a *Gustav*? Eight, if this well-known photograph is anything to go by. 5./JG 2's 'Black 12' ('*Kanonenboot*' Wk-Nr 27803) would be lost in action on 20 October 1943

To provide a two-seat trainer version of the Bf 109, the early months of 1944 saw the introduction of the G-12. These aircraft were simply conversions from other (non-pressurised) *Gustav* variants, and a requirement for some 500 G-12s was envisaged, but nothing like that number was delivered. Because the addition of the second seat behind the standard cockpit almost halved the internal fuel capacity (giving the G-12 an endurance of only 35 minutes!), 300-litre (660-gal) drop tanks were usually carried

But the G-12 was another instance of 'too little, too late' when the Luftwaffe tried to to halt the decline in training standards. After increasingly perfunctory basic training, the great majority of fighter pilots at this time transitioned straight to frontline single-seaters such as this *Gustav*, its school role indicated only by the three-digit fuselage numeral

themselves in an ever-steepening spiral of decline.

But all was yet far from lost, for new units were still being added to the Homeland's defensive order of battle. In the final months of 1943 two more Bf 109 *Gruppen* were transferred in from Italy. Major Franz Beyer's IV./JG 3 had only recently been activated, and early in 1944 it would commence re-equipment with heavily armed and armoured Fw 190s to become the Luftwaffe's first dedicated *Sturmgruppe*. In the interim, however, it had lost its *Kommandeur*. Knight's Cross holder Franz Beyer (already an 82-victory *Experte*) added just one more to his total during Defence of the Reich operations – a B-24 on 19 December 1943 – before being killed in action fighting Spitfires the following February.

The other *Gruppe* up from Italy was II./JG 53, led by Major Gerhard Michalski. The unit crossed the Alps only as far as Vienna, being initially tasked with the protection of Austria and southern Germany. They would be transferred further north to the central Rhine sector early in 1944. It was during the ensuing months up until the invasion of Normandy that 5. *Staffel's* Oberfeldwebel Herbert Rollwage claimed 12 of his 14 'heavies', and won the Knight's Cross while so doing.

But it was those self-same months which were to witness a rapid rise in the rate of attrition among the *Jagdwaffe's* experienced and irreplaceable unit leaders as the Eighth AF's heavy bombers – now enjoying the protection of Mustang escorts – launched a series of strikes aimed specifically at Germany's aircraft industry, and her fighter defences.

II./JG 3 had suffered a severe double blow even before 1943 was out, losing two *Gruppenkommandeure* in the space of a month. Shortly after midday on 3 November Major Kurt Brändle had claimed a pair of Thunderbolts which had formed part of the 378-strong fighter screen protecting a heavy US raid on Wilhelmshaven. Later that same afternoon the *Gruppe's* Schiphol base was subjected to a surprise attack by Ninth AF Marauders.

At a training establishment 'somewhere in Germany' a knot of overalled pupils (left) await their turn as a *Kette* of Bf 109Gs run up their engines. Close inspection will reveal that the machine in the centre is wearing a *Staffelkapitän*-style metal pennant on its aerial mast. Perhaps this photograph shows an instructor about to take up two trainee wingmen?

Scrambling after the rapidly retreating 'mediums', Brändle headed out over the North Sea. He failed to return, having fallen victim, it was presumed, to the bombers' Spitfire escort. No uncertainty surrounds the loss of Brändle's successor, Hauptmann Wilhelm Lemke, however. His *Gustav* was one of three shot down in action against P-47s carrying out a fighter sweep over the Netherlands on 4 December.

The fate of Brändle and Lemke was not only a foretaste of things to come in the run-up to D-Day, for it also encapsulates the dilemma facing the Luftwaffe High Command in their efforts to strengthen homeland defence. The training organisation was already beginning to show signs of strain. Hours were being cut and courses curtailed, and anything up to 30 trainees (the equivalent of an entire *Gruppe*) were being lost each month in fatal crashes. And those who completed their schooling and received postings to frontline units were of little immediate use, other than to make up numbers. Expertise had to be hard won, and many failed to survive their first few missions.

But the alternative – bringing in veteran units from other fronts – was equally, if not even more fraught. Although perhaps inevitable when pitted against a new and unfamiliar enemy who was rapidly gaining superiority both quantitatively and qualitatively, their losses (especially among the ranks of those with anything up to four years of combat experience behind them) left gaps that could not be filled.

II./JG 3's two *Kommandeure* were both wearers of the Oak Leaves, and each had amassed well over 100 Eastern front victories. Yet Brändle's two

The inadequacies of the Luftwaffe's training programme was beginning to tell. This gun-camera shot records the demise of a 9./JG 26 'Kanonenboot' near Gelsenkirchen on 5 November 1943. Although not visible here, the pilot, Unteroffizier Robert Pautner, had not jettisoned his drop tank when first attacked. Pautner bailed out wounded, and it is uncertain whether he returned to combat flying. He is certainly not credited with any victories. As for his assailant, Lt. Leroy Ista of the 352nd FS, Pautner's 'White 12' would be his only victim. While it was the few well-known 'Experten' and aces who amassed the kills and gained the glory, it was the likes of Pautner and Ista – the 'unsung heroes' – who, in their thousands, bore the main burden of the air war in the west

P-47s were his sole successes thereafter. Lemke had downed just one P-47 during his brief tenure of office, but to this must be added five kills claimed during his previous weeks as *Staffelkapitän* of 9./JG 3. Even so, eight Allied aircraft destroyed in defence of the Reich was poor recompense indeed against the loss of two such experienced combat veterans and formation leaders.

Nor was it just the relative newcomers from Russia who were now paying the price. Names of pilots who had already achieved considerable successes against the British and Americans were also beginning to appear on the casualty lists. Over half of the 20 heavy bombers claimed by Oberleutnant Willy Kientsch, *Staffelkapitän* of 6./JG 27, had been downed since his unit's return from the Mediterranean. He was killed on 29 January 1944.

Five weeks later, on 6 March – the day of the first large-scale daylight raid on Berlin – 7./JG 11's Oberleutnant Hugo Frey was shot down over Holland after accounting for no fewer than four B-17s in a single sortie. Although Frey's *Staffel* had re-equipped with Fw 190s by the time of this last notable achievement, it is possible that all the other 22 'heavies' credited to him were claimed on the *Gustav*. If this is the case, it would put Frey on a par with Hermann Staiger as the most successful Bf 109 heavy bomber *Experte* serving in Defence of the Reich.

But undoubtedly the most serious loss suffered by the *Jagdwaffe* in March 1944 was that of Oberstleutnant Wolf-Dietrich Wilcke, *Geschwaderkommodore* of JG 3. Wilcke's *Stab* had controlled all fighter operations over Stalingrad during the winter of 1942-43, and he personally had scored his 150th kill at the height of that battle. This had won him the Swords to his Oak Leaves, and an automatic ban on future operational flying. Wilcke nevertheless downed a further six Soviets before the *Stab's* return to Germany in the spring of 1943.

Another such was 4./JG 27's Unteroffizier Hans Seyringer, who had just one B-17 under his belt (brought down on 14 October 1943) before clashing with P-47s near Eindhoven on 30 January 1944. Seyringer was also forced to bail out wounded, later finding himself in hospital alongside the pilot of the P-47 he had just shot down! 'White 5' was the *Gustav* Seyringer was flying that day. Note the muzzle covers on the underwing cannon and the heavily oil-stained drop tank

Pictured earlier in his career as a Hauptmann and *Kommandeur* of III./JG 53 in Russia, Wolf-Dietrich Wilcke – another of the true greats of the *Jagdwaffe* – had been promoted to Oberst and *Kommodore* of JG 3 'Udet' by the time of his death in action against P-51s over the Reich on 23 March 1944

At the time of their *Kommodore's* loss III./JG 3 were based at Leipheim, to the west of Augsburg. Being serviced and refuelled in preparation for its next mission is 8. *Staffel's* 'Black 9'. Just visible above its numeral is the port wing of a Me 323 *'Gigant'*, the six-engined transport which was built at Messerschmitt's Leipheim facility

Wilcke then managed to refrain from combat for a whole year, but early in 1944, with JG 3 now fully committed in the defence of the Homeland, he again chose to ignore – or found a way to circumvent – the ban imposed upon him. In the space of little over a month he claimed six American aircraft: four heavy bombers and two fighters. The last of these (which fell on 23 March) was a P-51 which he turned into and shot down just as it was about to despatch his wingman.

Although the manoeuvre had put Wilcke at a severe disadvantage, it was typical of the man who was known throughout the *Jagdwaffe* as *'Fürst'* ('Prince') on account of his bearing, and innate sense of responsibility towards the welfare of his men. Almost inevitably, Wilcke's *Gustav* was immediately pounced upon by a second flight of Mustangs. The fighter crashed near Schöppenstedt, east of Brunswick.

The affection and respect felt for Wilcke by his peers was expressed by Oberst Günther Lützow, his predecessor as *Kommodore* of JG 3, who commented, 'He was a prince, a gentleman! And he will remain as such in our memories'.

Despite, or perhaps because of, the mounting list of losses, new units would continue to be fed into the Defence of the Reich organisation throughout 1944. A welcome infusion of strength right at the beginning of the year had been provided by the redeployment of JGs 300, 301 and 302. Originally created as single-seat *'Wilde Sau'* nightfighter units, these three *Geschwader* would henceforth operate predominantly by day (see *Osprey Aircraft of the Aces 9* and *20* for further details).

Although the majority of their component *Gruppen* were initially equipped with Bf 109s, which had served them well on nocturnal operations, it was with the Fw 190 that these newcomers gained most of their subsequent daylight successes. A number of Bf 109 pilots did amass considerable scores, however, including Hauptmann Heinrich Wurzer, *Staffelkapitän* of 1./JG 302 – all but three of his 26 victories were reportedly US 'heavies' by day. One of Wurzer's most experienced NCO pilots, Unteroffizier (later Oberfeldwebel) Willi Reschke also claimed 13 four-engined bombers (plus a P-51) while flying the Bf 109, and he later took his final tally to 27 after converting onto the Focke-Wulf.

This *'Kanonenboot'*, flown by Hauptmann Ludwig Franzisket, *Gruppenkommandeur* of I./JG 27, carries a most informative set of markings: the *Gruppe* badge on the cowling, *Kommandeur's* chevrons ahead of the cross and the white rudder of a formation leader. Less conspicuous – but of much more import – is the sage green band around the rear fuselage, which was introduced in January 1944 to indicate I./JG 27's current role as part of the Defence of the Reich organisation

A similar green band and white rudder are even harder to make out on the second *Gustav* in this line-up of machines only recently returned from the Mediterranean (note the dust filters on the other aircraft). 'Yellow 1' is the mount of Leutnant Dr Peter Werfft, *Staffelkapitän* of 9./JG 27

Four other *Gruppen* – two from the far north and two from the far south – were added to the Homeland's defensive line-up in the first half of 1944. I./JG 5 had, in fact, departed Norway late in 1943 for transfer, via a brief sojourn in Denmark, to south-east Europe. Here, based first in Rumania and then Bulgaria, they underwent their baptism of fire against large formations of American 'heavies' (of the Fifteenth AF, operating out of Italy) and lost their long-serving *Kommandeur*, Hauptmann Gerhard Wengel, to a P-38.

It was thus under Major Erich Gerlitz that I./JG 5 then arrived in Germany in February 1944 for re-equipment with Bf 109G-6/R6 *'Kanonenboote'*. The new *Kommandeur* did not survive long, however, for on 16 March he was shot down by P-47s east of Ulm. Command of the *Gruppe* then passed to Major Horst Carganico, an *Experte* from the Arctic front, where he had been *Gruppenkommandeur* of II./JG 5 for almost two years.

It therefore fell to Carganico's successor, Hauptmann Theo Weissenberger, to lead the aforementioned II./JG 5 down from the north upon that unit's deployment in Defence of the Reich some two months later. The *Gruppe* flew to Gardelegen, midway between Hannover and Berlin, towards the close of May 1944.

Meanwhile, the two remaining *Gruppen* of JG 27 still in the Mediterranean had also been recalled, III. and IV./JG 27 taking up station in Austria to guard the Reich's southern flanks. Between mid-March and the end of May 1944, and despite some heavy losses of their own, they exacted a considerable toll of Allied aircraft crossing the Alps from Italy. Several pilots of III. *Gruppe* claimed five or more heavy bombers, and at least two increased their scores by double figures during this period. Leutnant Dr Peter Werfft, *Staffelkapitän* of 9./JG 27, was credited with 11 'heavies', which took his overall total to 22, whilst 8./JG 27's Leutnant

Initially deployed in the southern extremities of Hitler's Reich, III. and IV./JG 27 were tasked with combating incursions across the Alps by US bombers flying up from Italy. Whether a victim of the *Gruppen's Gustavs* or not, this natural metal B-17G of the Fifteenth AF's 2nd BG is one that won't be making the return trip to Amendola

Alexander Ottnad went one better by adding a dozen four-engined bombers – plus a single P-51 – to his previous score of five.

By contrast, almost half of IV./JG 27's kills were made up of fighters, and this would seem to suggest that they were being employed as a *'leichte' Gruppe*, charged with engaging the bombers' escorting fighters. Their highest scorer was another of those experienced NCOs who so often proved to be the bedrock of a successful unit. Holder of the Knight's Cross, and already an *Experte* on both the Arctic and Mediterranean fronts, Feldwebel Heinrich Bartels had begun Defence of the Reich duties with 73 victories to his credit. Now, in the space of just over a month, he added another 12 – all fighters, and all American, except for a trio of Spitfires downed in four hectic minutes early on the morning of 23 April.

While all this was going on far to the south, those true veterans of the war in the west, the Channel-based JGs 2 and 26, had been bearing the full brunt of the growing might of combined Anglo-American air power. Unlike the *Jagdgruppen* stationed deep within Germany's borders, theirs was a frontline campaign constantly being fought on two levels. For not only did they have to contend with high-flying US 'heavies' attacking strategic targets within their own areas (from the U-boat pens in the west to airfields and industrial objectives in the east) and beyond, they also had to oppose the swelling tide of tactical strikes being mounted by the RAF and the US Ninth AF as the coastal regions of north-west Europe were 'softened up' for the forthcoming invasion.

On 16 January 1944 JG 2 had claimed its 2000th enemy aircraft destroyed. Including, as it did, 350 four-engined heavy bombers and 200 twin-engined mediums, this total reflected both the severity and the variety of the *Geschwader's* operations. JG 26 attained its 2000th less than six weeks later on 25 February.

On 2 March 1944 Major Kurt Bühligen, *Gruppenkommandeur* of the Bf 109-equipped II./JG 2 currently based at Creil, north of Paris, was awarded the Oak Leaves for 96 kills. This made him top scorer against the Western Allies at this time, having scored one more than Oberstleutnant

Far to the north – based at Rotenburg, between Bremen and Hamburg – II./JG 3 'Udet' was just one of the *Gruppen* defending the vital North Sea coastal belt. Seen here are two of 4. *Staffel's* NCO pilots, Oberfeldwebel Helmut Rüffler (left) and Gefreiter Hans Kupka, in front of the latter's 'White 13'. Kupka parachuted wounded from this machine on 21 February 1944. Knight's Cross winner Rüffler, himself shot down five times, was credited with eight heavy bombers among his dozen victories in the west

Josef Priller, *Kommodore* of JG 26. Bühligen's tally, however, is slightly misleading in that it includes at least 40 victories claimed during II./JG 2's deployment to Tunisia on Fw 190s. One or more of Bühligen's 24 'heavies' were likewise downed over Africa and/or while flying the Fw 190, which made him yet another possible claimant for the title of equal top Bf 109 heavy bomber *Experte*!

Third highest scorer in the west at this juncture was III./JG 2's Oberleutnant Josef Wurmheller with 88 kills (plus nine in the east). But both 'Pips' Priller and 'Sepp' Wurmheller had converted to the Fw 190 months earlier.

Meanwhile, further to the west, JGs 2 and 26 were fighting a two-level war against the USAF and the RAF. Both could be equally hazardous, but if caught at altitude a *Gustav* pilot might at least be able to take to his parachute . . .

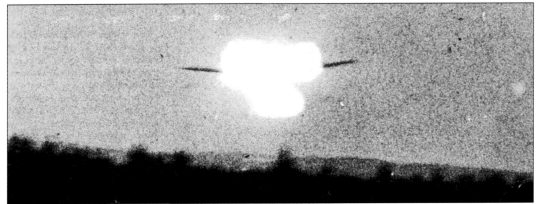

Although relatively little known outside the tight-knit ranks of the *Jagdwaffe*, Kurt Bühligen was one of its greats. From groundcrew beginnings, he had volunteered for flying training and had graduated early in 1940. Posted to JG 2 as an NCO pilot at the start of the Battle of Britain in July of that year, he would remain with the *Geschwader* throughout the war, rising to become its tenth and final *Kommodore*, with the Swords added to his Oak Leaves and an eventual total of 112 victories – all scored against western opponents.

Having flown the Bf 109 and the Fw 190, Bühligen was familiar with

. . . whereas, at ground level, he stood very little chance of survival

Portrayed later in the war as an Oberleutnant, and wearing the Swords to the Oak Leaves of his knight's Cross, Kurt Bühligen was undoubtedly one of JG 2's most successful pilots throughout the *Geschwader's* long years of campaigning against the British and Americans. All 112 of his kills (including 24 heavy bombers) were scored against the Western Allies

Late in 1943 the *Erla-Haube* (or 'Erla hood', so called, it is believed, after the original manufacturer) had begun to appear on the Bf 109G. This clear canopy offered the pilot a greatly improved field of vision. Here, an *Erla*-canopied *Gustav* of III./JG 26 taxies out at Lille-North in the spring of 1944 ready for its next mission. Note, once again, the sun umbrella clamps beneath the windscreen, and yet another oily drop tank

the foibles and strengths of both. The latter's propensity to flick sharply over on to one wing during certain manoeuvres was well known and employed by many Fw 190 pilots to extricate themselves from a tight corner. The Bf 109 possessed no such inbuilt, but propitious, flaw. Many of its pilots, Bühligen revealed, therefore fell back on a tactic of their own devising for use in an emergency.

They would fly with their machine trimmed slightly tail heavy, keeping the nose down by constant forward pressure on the stick. In moments of crisis the stick could be pulled back and the nose would immediately point upwards without the momentary 'mushing' which could easily prove fatal in a dogfight.

Bühligen is on record with an even more telling statement. 'All the pilots who came to me from the Eastern front fell on the Western front.' Casualties among arrivals from the other theatres were, and indeed would continue to be, a huge drain on Defence of the Reich resources. Losses of experienced and hard to replace formation leaders were becoming ever more grievous – four were killed in the month leading up to D-Day alone.

Since II./JG 3's return from Russia, one of its most successful pilots had been Oberleutnant Leopold Münster, *Kapitän* of 5. *Staffel*. By April 1944 he had added 13 heavy bombers and a pair each of P-38s and P-51s to his previous score of 76. On 8 May 1944 Münster's *Gustav* was just one of some 400 *Jagdwaffe* machines sent up against American formations totalling almost four times that number. Penetrating the heavy fighter screen, Münster quickly claimed a B-17, only to be killed minutes later when he collided with a B-24. The Liberator exploded in mid-air, and Münster's Bf 109 and the remains of his 95th, and final, victim fell to earth south of the enemy's objective, Brunswick. Oberleutnant Münster was posthumously honoured with the Oak Leaves.

On 27 May 60-victory *Experte*, and Arctic front veteran, Major Horst Carganico – the recently-appointed *Kommandeur* of I./JG 5 – lost his life when he hit high-tension wires while attempting a forced-landing after action against US bombers over France.

Forty-eight hours later the officer who had succeeded *'Fürst'* Wilcke as *Kommodore* of JG 3 was likewise killed in a landing accident. Major Friedrich-Karl Müller (not to be confused with the top-scoring nightfighter *Experte* of exactly the

Three of the experienced formation leaders to be killed in the month leading up to D-Day are seen on this spread. Oberleutnant Leopold Münster, *Staffelkapitän* of 5./JG 3, casts an expert's eye at the sky above his Schiphol base. 'Poldi' Münster would lose his life in a mid-air collision with a US bomber on 8 May

same name – see *Osprey Aircraft of the Aces 20 - German Nightfighter Aces of World War 2* for further details) had opened his scoresheet during the Battle of France as a member of Mölder's III./JG 53. By the time he was appointed commander of IV./JG 3 in Defence of the Reich in February 1944, *'Tutti'* Müller was wearing Oak Leaves and had amassed 117 kills.

During his month at the head of IV. *Gruppe*, he added five heavy bombers to that number. Another 17 (plus a P-51) followed during his nine weeks as *Geschwaderkommodore*. With 22 four-engined heavies to his credit, Friedrich-Karl Müller is yet another strong contender in the top Bf 109 'bomber-killer' stakes.

But one casualty overshadowed all others during that month of May. Ranking alongside such names as Mölders and Galland as one of the most outstanding combat leaders ever produced by the *Jagdwaffe*, Walter Oesau's career had begun with the *Condor Legion* in Spain, where he had downed nine Republican aircraft. *Staffelkapitän* of 7./JG 51 upon the outbreak of the war, Oesau later served as a *Gruppenkommandeur* in both JGs 51 and 3, before assuming command of JG 2 after the death of Balthasar in July 1941.

Newly decorated with the Swords to his Oak leaves, and with 86 wartime victories to his credit upon arrival, Walter Oesau headed JG 2 for two gruelling years. Despite the ban on further operational flying which accompanied his 'century' on 26 October 1941, the Lancaster Oesau famously shot down in 'self-defence' the following April (his 101st) was not the last victim he

claimed. He added at least another four, it is believed, before his appointment as *Jafü Bretagne* (Fighter Leader Britanny) in the summer of 1943.

This unwelcome staff position was relatively brief, for on 12 November 1943 Oberst Walter Oesau returned to an operational posting as *Kommodore* of JG 1. Shortly thereafter the ban on combat flying was temporarily lifted (or again tacitly ignored until discovery?), for in the two months between January and the beginning of March 1944 he claimed another string of successes, including nine heavy bombers and four fighters. Two more months were to elapse before his next kill – number 118 was a P-47 shot down north of Hannover on 8 May. It was to be his last victory.

On 11 May the Eighth AF launched a major effort, with close on 1000 B-17s and B-24s being escorted, and supported, by more than that number of fighters on raids against rail targets in eastern France and Belgium. Among the fighters opposing them were JG 1, including the *Stabsschwarm* led by Oberst Oesau.

References again differ as to the subsequent course of events. It is generally accepted, however, that the *Stabsschwarm* became split up as they attempted to approach an American formation high over the Ardennes. Oesau's wingman then reported damage to his machine and he was instructed to break away by the *Kommodore*. Left on his own, Oesau was attacked by four P-38s (some sources quote the involvement of P-51s). Using all those flying skills amassed during years of combat, the Oberst defended himself furiously in a swirling dogfight which 'lasted for 20 minutes, and descended from 28,000 ft (8500 m) to tree-top level'.

The end, when it came, was swift. Oesau was apparently preparing to make an emergency landing when a final burst of fire struck the cockpit area of his *Gustav*. The fighter smashed into the ground ten kilometres (six miles) to the south-west of the Belgian town of St Vith and Oesau's body was thrown clear. It was later recovered yards from the wreckage.

Jagdgeschwader 1 was subsequently given the title 'Oesau' in honour of its fallen *Kommodore* – an accolade to a wartime combat leader only previously bestowed upon JG 51 'Mölders'. And although other *Geschwaderkommodore* would be killed in action before the end of hostilities, none reflected the changing fortunes of the Luftwaffe's fighter forces more graphically than the loss of Oberst Walter Oesau.

Hitherto, despite the lengthening casualty lists, the *Jagdwaffe* had managed to hold its own in the west. But in less than four weeks the first Allied troops would be storming ashore on the Normandy beaches, and the long retreat to final surrender would be underway.

NORMANDY AND THE DEFENCE OF THE REICH

lthough, by the spring of 1944, the German High Command was fully aware that a cross-Channel invasion was imminent, it was unsure of the exact point of assault. Elaborate Allied decoy schemes had succeeded in leading many to believe that the invasion fleet would cross the Channel via the Straits of Dover, where it was at its narrowest, and that enemy troops would land in the Pas de Calais area. Others saw the flat beaches of Normandy as a more likely location.

Hitler remained undecided long after Anglo-American forces had gained a firm foothold. His well-known 'intuition' told him that the

Once the Allies had landed in France it was a different story for the incoming *Jagdgruppen*. II./JG 3's destination on D+1 was Evreux. This tall-tailed G-6 ('Black Chevron 1' – possibly the mount of *Gruppen-Adjutant* Oberleutnant Max-Bruno Fischer) seeks what shelter it can, hiding its white Defence of the Reich band beneath a tree in a distinctly rolling meadow

III./JG 1 spent its first few days in France at Beauvais, north of Paris, before retiring to the less easy to find (and bomb!) La Fère. It is here that 9. *Staffel's* 'Yellow 2' is seen during its landing approach. Possibly a recent replacement aircraft (note the lack of JG 1's red Reich's Defence fuselage band), Wk-Nr 413553 was another tall-tailed G-6. A wounded Oberfähnrich Lothar Lutz would bail out of this machine during a dogfight with Spitfires on 30 July

Once on the ground, it was imperative that the Luftwaffe's fighters be quickly concealed. While two youthful looking pilots discuss a recent sortie, a crowd of mechanics push a *Gustav* into a gap among the trees

Normandy landings of 6 June were nothing but a gigantic feint. Despite the urgent pleas of his ground commanders, he refused to release *Panzer* divisions from other sectors to contain the beachheads. By the time he reluctantly agreed to their transfer, it was too late.

By contrast, the Luftwaffe's reaction was remarkably swift. Within hours the whole Defence of the Reich edifice, so painstakingly put together over the past months, had been torn apart. By the evening of 9 June no fewer than 15 *Jagdgruppen* – all but four of them flying Bf 109s – had departed the Homeland for the threatened Western front. Their destinations had been meticulously marked on staff situation maps. Those *Gruppen* intended primarily for the *Jabo* role were to be deployed on airfields between the Loire and the Seine. The bulk of the force would be based further back along the line Paris-Creil-St Quentin, while three *Gruppen* would be located yet further to the rear in eastern France, as aerial 'longstops' against possible deeper Allied incursions.

But, as so often in the past, the reality of the situation on the ground – or, more accurately, in the air – rendered all this careful planning completely redundant. Such was the Allies' overwhelming superiority (something approaching 20:1 in fighter strength alone) that the *Jagdgruppen* soon had to abandon their assigned bases, which were being bombed into rubble, and seek shelter where they could on small, dispersed and heavily camouflaged landing strips. Yet even here they were not safe from the roving hordes of enemy fighter-bombers, which pounced on the slightest sign of activity. By the end of June the Luftwaffe had lost over 350 aircraft destroyed or damaged on the ground, the majority of them fighters.

For many of the pilots, who had only just begun to get to grips with the high-altitude anti-bomber air war over the Reich, the additional low-level dimension dictated by their opponents during much of the Normandy fighting simply proved too much. During the last three weeks of June over 170 of them were killed in action. Inevitably, perhaps, it was the

But it would soon be time again to face the overwhelming weight of Allied air power. A late model *Gustav* (note the FuG 16ZY antenna beneath the port wing) is readied for a forthcoming mission . . .

younger pilots, inexperienced and inadequately trained, who suffered the most. Luftwaffe reports indicated that 25-30 such youngsters could be expected to be lost for every *alte Hase* who was brought down.

The latter were even being officially 'safeguarded'. Such had been the rate of loss among near indispensable formation leaders in the months leading up to D-Day, that the High Command now sought to restrict their flying unless they were adequately protected. An order signed by *Reichsmarschall* Göring, dated 5 July, laid down the conditions – on a rising scale, *Staffelkapitäne* could only fly if accompanied by five other aircraft, *Gruppenkommandeure*, 15, and *Geschwaderkommodoren* 44!

Within a fortnight of their arrival in France many *Jagdgruppen* had been reduced to single figure strength, with some being unable to field

. . . from which increasing numbers were failing to return. British intelligence officers pick over the remains of 6./JG 11's 'Yellow 7', whose crash-landing near Creully, some eight kilometres (five miles) inland from the beachhead, on D+1 had been brought to an abrupt halt by a sturdy stone wall. Pilot Unteroffizier Rudolf Strosetzki survived his brush with American P-47s (and this even closer acquaintance with the art of an anonymous Norman stonemason) to become a prisoner of war

The *Jagdwaffe* suffered a more unusual loss in the early hours of 21 July. Leutnant Horst Prenzel, *Staffelkapitän* of 1./JG 301, had taken off from Epinoy on a '*Wilde Sau*' sortie over the invasion area. After an uneventful two-and-a-half-hour patrol he put down at 0240 hrs on an airfield in Belgium – or so he thought. In fact, he had landed at RAF Manston, in Kent (a second '*Wilde Sau*' *Gustav* also crash-landed in error at the airfield that same night). Here, his G-6/U2 'White 16' (Wk-Nr 412951) is pictured both on the morning after its unscheduled arrival, and in the later colours of its new owners. Note the RAF serial, TP814, applied over the rust-red aft fuselage band of the early '*Wilde Sau*' units. Following its surprise acquisition, the RAF flew the aircraft firstly to RAE Farnborough, where it was tested by Sqn Ldr R J Falk, before being passed to the Air Fighting Development Unit (AFDU) at RAF Wittering on 31 August 1944. Here, it flew comparative performance trials with the Mustang III and Spitfire IX and XIV. It was also scheduled to fly against the Tempest V, but was written off in a take-off accident at Wittering on 23 November 1944

more than a *Schwarm* of four fighters. Although the losses in men and machines were constantly being made good, the replacements fared even worse. But, despite all their difficulties, the Bf 109s managed to claim a large number of Allied aircraft in return. Success rates varied from *Gruppe* to *Gruppe* but, again unsurprisingly, it was the small core of surviving older hands – several familiar names among them – who scored the most.

Leutnant Herbert Rollwage, 5./JG 53's *Viermot-Experte*, narrowly missed becoming a Normandy ace by adding just four US aircraft (a B-26 and a trio of fighters) to his list of kills between June and August. Major Ernst Düllberg, *Gruppenkommandeur* of III./JG 27, also claimed four victories (all fighters) during the same period. II./JG 11's *Kommandeur*, Hauptmann Walter Krupinski, went one better; downing five US fighters during June and July. This brought 'Count Punski's' overall total to just five short of an incredible double 'century', the vast majority of his earlier successes having been scored with JG 52 in the east. Wounded in August, Walter Krupinski would claim just two more victims (a Spitfire and a P-51) while leading III./JG 26 in the autumn, before joining JV 44.

Another Eastern front veteran was Oberleutnant Hans Waldmann, whose 4./JG 52 was redesignated to become 8./JG 3 towards the close of the Normandy campaign. Waldmann's eight August victories took his score to 132, and like Krupinski, he too transitioned to jets during the final months of the war; downing a brace of Mustangs while flying the Me 262, before being killed in a mid-air collision in March 1945 (see *Osprey Aircraft of the Aces 17 - German Jet Aces* for further details). It was during August, too, that the indefatigable Heinz Knoke, newly appointed

75

Gruppenkommandeur of III./JG 1, also claimed eight victories, thereby taking his current tally of western victims to 33.

At least four pilots lengthened their list of kills by double figures during clashes over Normandy. IV./JG 27's veteran NCO, Feldwebel Heinrich Bartels (already an *Experte* on both the Arctic and Mediterranean fronts), downed 11 Allied fighters in just 12 days between 14 and 25 June.

A more recent arrival from the far north was Leutnant August Mors of I./JG 5. He, too, accounted for 11 enemy fighters in a matter of days, before taking off on 6 August with two wingmen (in the *Gruppe's* last three serviceable *Gustavs!*) to attack an approaching formation of heavy bombers. Mors claimed one of the B-24s – his only *Viermot* – before himself being hit and badly wounded. Although he succeeded in baling out, he died of his wounds 48 hours later. August Mors was honoured with a posthumous Knight's Cross in October.

Having joined JG 26 before the war, the now Major Klaus Mietusch, *Kommandeur* of III. *Gruppe* since July 1943, was a proven Western front *Experte*, albeit one who was seemingly dogged by misfortune. He had been a prisoner of the French for a short spell in 1940, had been wounded on at least four occasions, and had been shot down ten times! However, apart from brief deployments to the Mediterranean and Russia as a member, and latterly the *Staffelkapitän*, of 7./JG 26, all his victories had been achieved in the west against the British and Americans. During the Normandy campaign a dozen such successes between June and August had raised his total to 74. His 75th, and final, kill came after III./JG 26's withdrawal from France when he downed a P-51 north-west of Düsseldorf on 17 September. Succumbing to another Mustang only minutes after his last victory, Mietusch would also be honoured posthumously; his Oak Leaves being awarded in November.

But possibly the most successful Bf 109 pilot of all those involved in the Normandy fighting was Hauptmann Theodor Weissenberger, the new *Gruppenkommandeur* of I./JG 5. He is credited with no fewer than 25

Despite the high summer's high losses, the *Jagdwaffe* continued to give of its best. A *'Kanonenboot'* gets a final check-over before leaving the sanctuary of the woods

An *Erla*-canopied G-6 (possibly of III./JG 26 at Villacoublay) kicks up a cloud of dust as it taxies between roadworks to get to the runway. Just visible below the spinner are the (white-knuckled?) hands of a groundcrewman clutching the leading-edge of the starboard wing – presumably he is there to guide the pilot past the obstacles

enemy aircraft destroyed over France in a space of seven weeks. This remarkable achievement culminated in his 200th victory – one of a pair of Spitfires brought down south of Rouen on 25 July. In fact, the little-known Weissenberger's entire wartime career was remarkable. It had begun on Bf 110s in the Arctic, where 23 kills quickly confirmed him as a *Zerstörer-Experte*. After converting to the Bf 109, another 152 victories made him an Eastern front ace many times over, whilst his 25 Normandy successes also established his position as a Western front *Experte*. Weissenberger would end the war as *Geschwaderkommodore* of the Me 262-equipped JG 7, with eight further kills making him a *bona fide* jet ace!

But such individual achievements, however noteworthy, could not disguise the fact that the *Jagdwaffe* in the west was now in irreversible decline. Towards the end of August 1944 the surviving remnants of those *Gruppen* which had been thrown into France three months earlier – together with those two long-term residents of the Channel coast, JGs 2

Few, if any, were more successful in the air war over Normandy than I./JG 5's Hauptmann Theodor Weissenberger, whose 25 kills during the campaign took his overall score to 200. Here, the event is duly celebrated at the *Gruppe's* Frières base, with Weissenberger – in the dark shirt, wearing the Knight's Cross and Oak Leaves – almost lost in a sea of congratulatory garlands

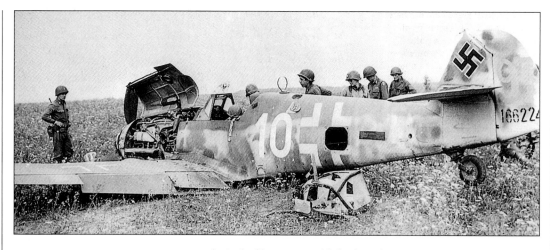

When the *Jagdwaffe* departed France it left behind much evidence of its passing, including this G-6 of II./JG 3. Abandoned after a wheels-up landing at Nogent-le-Roi early in August, 'White 10' (Wk-Nr 166224) is now the subject of scrutiny by a group of US soldiers. Note the shattered *Erla* hood on the ground below the fuselage cross

and 26 – had begun to trickle back to the Homeland. They formed just a small part of the mass exodus of units retreating from the Western front.

Meanwhile, what of the single-engined fighter forces which had been retained throughout the summer in Defence of the Reich? These initially comprised the bulk of the ex-'*Wilde Sau*' units – two heavily-armoured Fw 190 *Sturmgruppen* (see *Osprey Aircraft of the Aces 9*) and a trio of Bf 109 *Gruppen* (II./JG 5, II./JG 27 and III./JG 53). Although not subjected to quite the same amount of harassment on the ground as their French-based brethren, theirs was otherwise a very similar story – some appreciable successes, but offset by a steady drain of casualties. It was a war of attrition the depleted *Jagdwaffe* could not win. In July 1944 alone, Defence of the Reich units claimed 329 aircraft destroyed for the loss of 341 of their own. But whereas the former constituted just a fraction of the enemy's strength (and could be quickly replaced), the latter represented the equivalent of almost the entire Homeland single-seater defence force.

Numerically, in fact, the Defence of the Reich organisation was 'wiped out' many times over before the final collapse. And while the diminishing band of experienced combat leaders continued to give of their best – III./JG 53's top scorer between July and September 1944, for example, was *Kommandeur* Major Franz 'Old Father' Götz with just six kills – the last nine months of hostilities in the west degenerated into a steady catalogue of losses as the *Jagdwaffe*, by now a force chronically short of fuel, and made up predominantly of idealistic, by sketchily trained, youngsters, sought desperately to stave off defeat.

The return of the shattered remnants of the Normandy *Gruppen* brought no immediate relief to the embattled Defence of the Reich units, for it would be several long weeks before many of the former would be ready for frontline service again. Consequently, one final round of reinforcements was added to Homeland defence in the late summer/early autumn of 1944. The majority – elements of JGs 4 and 77 – were withdrawn from the southern and south-eastern perimeters of Hitler's rapidly shrinking *Festung Europa* ('Fortress Europe'). But two 'new' Bf 109 *Gruppen* in I. and III./JG 76 were ex-Zerstörer units (I./ZG 76 and II./ZG 1 respectively), which had been all but annihilated in recent Defence of the Reich operations and had now converted to single-seaters.

A bri rry of redesignations shortly thereafter, which saw, amongst

The retreat from France did not halt the slaughter, as witness this pair of unfortunates, which were both obviously taking hits from pursuing Allied fighters. Curiously, the photo of the machine showing strikes on its port wing (below – the combination of long, fixed tailwheel leg and triple Defence of the Reich fuselage bands suggesting, perhaps, a late-war G-10 of JG 4?) was not released by the US Department of Defense until June 1951, when it was used to promote civil defence awareness in mainland America!

others, I. and III./JG 76 become IV./JG 300 and IV./JG 53. This brought some semblance of uniformity to the Defence of the Reich's by now over-complicated order of battle, but achieved little else of practical value.

It certainly did nothing to affect the daily lot of the *Jagdwaffe*. And nothing served better to illustrate the latter's seeming impotence at this stage of the campaign in the west than the long, vulnerable trains of unarmed Allied transport aircraft and glider-tugs which flew low over German-occupied Holland on 17 September at the start of Operation *Market Garden*, the airborne battle for Arnhem. Their losses *en route* were remarkably light, and those they did suffer were, without exception, reportedly the victims of anti-aircraft fire. Although the Luftwaffe High Command hastily organised three large *Gefechtsverbände* ('Battle-groups', together totalling at least eight *Jagdgruppen*) to combat the landings, fighter opposition to the initial assault, and the follow-up supply flights, was conspicuous by its absence.

There were many reasons for the *Jagdwaffe*'s failure at Arnhem, but lack of aircraft was not one of them. That September, production reached an all-time high, with no fewer than 3013 single-engined fighters alone being delivered to the Luftwaffe (newly built, or returned after repair).

In mid-October 1944 the first examples of the final major production model of the Bf 109, the K-4, began to reach the Defence of the Reich *Jagdgruppen*. And although it is estimated that over 1500 Bf 109K-4s had been produced by the war's end, it was all too little, too late. The Luftwaffe no longer had the infrastructure to support them, the fuel to power them, or the trained pilots to fly them. Some twenty *Jagdgruppen* in all would operate the K-4 alongside their late-model *Gustavs*, but only a handful – four or five at most – would convert entirely onto the new variant, and some of these for only short periods.

Given the above, plus the fact that many *Jagdgruppen* were transferred to the Eastern front in January 1945, it is difficult to say exactly how

Although the exact dates and locations are unknown, the combination of *Erla* hood and spiralled spinner on this G-6, coupled with the obviously dry and dusty conditions, would seem to suggest that it was operating from a makeshift field 'somewhere in the west' during the late summer/early autumn of 1944. The pilot enjoys the benefit of a 'wingman' to guide him across an open patch of ground (like its Spitfire counterpart, the forward field of vision from a taxying Bf 109 was notoriously poor)

'White 7' of III./JG 3's 9. *Staffel*, a G-14 (Wk-Nr 462919), flew fighter cover for the Fw 190 *'Sturmböcke'* of IV. *Gruppe* in the autumn of 1944. Note the overpainted national insignia (and the Fw 190 tail visible immediately above the darkened *Balkenkreuz*)

many true Bf 109K aces emerged during the chaotic closing months of the war. Certainly very few. Among the 'major' operators of the K-4 were the third *Gruppen* of JGs 27, 53 and 77. And whereas III./JG 77 ended the war in the east, the other two *Gruppen* remained in the west until the final collapse. Both produced strong claimants to Bf 109K 'acedom'.

Leutnant Emil Clade, *Staffelkapitän* of 12./JG 27, who was promoted to Oberleutnant and command of III./JG 27 in February 1945, scored exactly five kills between December 1944 and February 1945, thereby taking his final total to 27. One of Clade's pilots, Feldwebel – later Fahnenjunker-Feldwebel (Officer Candidate) – Walter Arnold, also claimed five Allied aircraft destroyed from December onwards, the last, an Auster brought down on 2 April, raising his overall tally to eight. As III./JG 27 had converted fully to the K-4 by the end of October 1944, both Clade and Arnold must be presumed to have achieved their five final kills apiece on the new model Messerschmitt.

There are also two contenders from the ranks of III./JG 53. *Gruppenkommandeur* Hauptmann Siegfried Luckenbach is credited with five kills during February and March 1945, whilst the *Kapitän* of his 11. *Staffel*, Leutnant Günther Landt, had already claimed a trio of P-47s in February 1945, before colliding with a Mustang during a dogfight west of Stuttgart on the 23rd of that month – slightly wounded, Landt baled out of his stricken K-4, Wk-Nr 332660. By the beginning of March he was back in action, bringing down three more Allied fighters, plus a B-26,

Despite being taken after III./JG 3's transfer to the east in January 1945, this heavily-retouched photo of 11. *Staffel's* 'Yellow 1' (Wk-Nr 334176) is included to illustrate the salient features of the K-4 – the 'unbulged' upper cowling associated with the DB 605D engine, mainwheel doors, repositioned dorsal fuel filler cap (indicated by the warning triangle), which was moved forward one frame and displaced the D/F loop to its rear, and long-legged retractable tailwheel

between then and 24 April. Landt's last seven kills (out of a total of 22) could well make him the top scoring Bf 109K of them all.

In addition to those named above, many other pilots, already successful on the *Gustav*, undoubtedly flew the K-model as well (unlike the earlier variants, the last member of the prolific Bf 109 family was not in service long enough to become known by a phonetic initial, although both *Karl* and *Konrad* have appeared in print in post-war histories). But talk of Bf 109K aces in the closing weeks of the war is premature.

1000 VICTORIES

On 5 October 1944 the OKL had proudly announced that II. *Jagdkorps* had just achieved its 1000th victory in the west since the opening of the second front on 6 June. It neglected to spell out the casualties suffered over the same period. I. *Jagdkorps*, responsible for the Defence of the Reich, was also now paying an even heavier price for its successes against the Eighth AF. On 1 November the *Korps'* strength included 347 single-engined day fighters. Within 24 hours it had lost nearly a third of them. Massed raids by over 1100 'heavies' on synthetic oil installations in central Germany on 2 November cost the defenders 70 pilots killed and a further 28 wounded.

But *General der Jagdflieger* Adolf Galland (whose three-year tenure of office was soon to end amid charges of treason, his outspoken, but justified, criticism of the Luftwaffe's leadership finally becoming more than the *Reichsmarschall* could tolerate) had one last trick up his sleeve. Galland had been hoarding what little fuel there was, and preparing his fighter units for what he termed *'der grosse Schlag'* ('the big blow'). This was to be the largest, and most decisive, air battle of the European air war, far eclipsing the *Jagdwaffe's* victories over Schweinfurt.

In the next spell of favourable weather, every available fighter (Galland envisaged some 2000 machines!) would be sent up against the American 'heavies'. The intention was to shoot down 400-500 bombers for the loss of about 400 fighters and, possibly, 100-150 pilots. Such a blow would shatter the Eighth AF's ability, and will, to continue their daylight air offensive, Galland argued.

But he was outranked by the one man whose word was law in Nazi Germany. The Führer had plans of his own for a 'big blow'. Galland's carefully husbanded force, trained in high-altitude anti-bomber tactics, was ordered to to support a major new land offensive on the Western front.

Belying their youthful appearance, it was pilots such as these – of II./JG 53, pictured at Malmsheim in November 1944 – who kept the *Jagdwaffe* in the air until the bitter end. Arguably the youngest looking of them all, Leutnant Karl Broo (at right), claimed his fifth kill – a Spitfire – during Operation *Bodenplatte*. Appointed *Staffelkapitän* of 5./JG 53 in March 1945, his 13th, and final, victory was a P-51 downed south-west of Ulm on 20 April – less than three weeks before Germany's surrender

For Hitler was now preparing to repeat the surprise move which had won him the Battle of France four years earlier by bursting out of the Ardennes and racing for the sea, thus cutting the enemy's ground forces in two.

The 'Battle of the Bulge', as it has since become known, was launched on 16 December 1944. Meteorologically, it was the very opposite of Galland's aborted *grosse Schlag*, relying on poor weather to keep the Allies' superior air power pinned to the ground. The adverse conditions apparently did not prevent the *Jagdwaffe* from playing its part, for on 19 December *Generalmajor* Dietrich Peltz, the local GOC, pronounced himself pleased with the way air operations (primarily ground support) had been conducted during the first two days of the counter-offensive.

But with the weather starting to clear on 22 December, and Allied air superiority beginning to make itself felt again, *Generalmajor* Peltz soon changed his tune. Within the week he was complaining of pilots' breaking off their attacks without good reason, jettisoning their extra fuel tanks, and heading back to base. Such incidents seemed to be confirmed by a signal picked up by the Allied intercept service. In it, Oberst Gustav Rödel, *Geschwaderkommodore* of JG 27, estimated that 20 per cent of his pilots had behaved in exactly this way on 23 December, and he threatened to court-martial any who did so again in future.

23 December also happened to be the date of Oberfeldwebel Heinrich Bartel's 99th, and final victory – a P-47 downed near Bonn. IV./JG 27's highest scorer, who had been nominated for the Oak Leaves, failed to return from this mission. The remains of Bartels, and his *Gustav*, would not be found for nearly a quarter of a century. It was on this day, too, that a combined force of Bf 109s and Fw 190s of JG 11 claimed no fewer than 28 B-26s, plus a clutch of US fighters, over the Moselle Valley.

In the light of the previously mentioned, intercepted, signal, it appears

that Gustav Rödel, himself a leading *Experte* against the western allies (his final score of 98 included one solitary Soviet victim), preferred the 'stick' to the 'carrot' when attempting to persuade his inexperienced youngsters to display similar aggression!

By the last week of December the German counter-offensive had been blunted. The supporting *Jagdwaffe* received a severe mauling as the weather improved, and within just 48 hours they had lost some 200 pilots, including four *Gruppenkommandeure* and seven *Staffelkapitäne*. Yet it was now that Galland's proposal for a 'big blow' against the Allied air forces was resuscitated. It would not be struck in the air against the Eighth AF, however, but on the ground against the Allies' forward tactical airfields in the Low Countries and France. Nor would it consist of the 2000 fighters hoped for by Galland, but something less than half that number – still an amazing achievement – made up of 33 *Jagdgruppen,* 19 of them equipped with the Bf 109.

Operation *Bodenplatte* ('Baseplate'), launched on New Year's Day 1945, was to sound the death knell for the *Jagdwaffe* in the west. The material damage wrought against ground targets by the largely inexperienced attackers in this final folly was minimal and speedily made good. By contrast, their own losses – compounded by 'friendly' flak over their own lines from gunners unused to seeing so many Luftwaffe aircraft in the air at one time – were grievous: 214 pilots killed or missing, plus 18 wounded. Among the casualties were many formation leaders, including three Bf 109 *Gruppenkommandeure.*

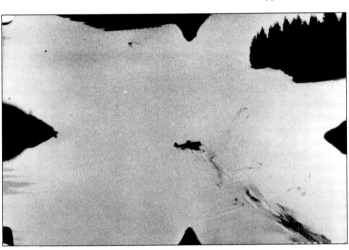

Once the weather had cleared, the latter half of the Ardennes counter-offensive inevitably resulted in further heavy losses. This short gun camera sequence encapsulates the fate of the German fighter force in the west – although this particular Bf 109 pilot was luckier than many. He managed to jettison his blazing drop tank and pull off a successful belly landing in the snow

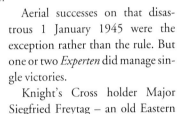

Aerial successes on that disastrous 1 January 1945 were the exception rather than the rule. But one or two *Experten* did manage single victories.

Knight's Cross holder Major Siegfried Freytag – an old Eastern front and Mediterranean campaigner, currently acting *Kommodore* of JG 77 – brought down a Spitfire during the course of his *Geschwader's* attack on Antwerp-Deurne for his 102nd, and last, kill of the war. A more recent Knight's Cross recipient, Leutnant Oskar Zimmermann, *Staffelkapitän* of 9./JG 3, claimed a Tempest over Eindhoven, JG 3's assigned objective. Zimmermann would end the war with 48 kills, 14 of them four-engined.

Oberfeldwebel Eduard Isken of 13./JG 53, a long-serving and highly experienced NCO pilots whose operational career had begun in 1940, was approaching Metz-Frescaty (the only one of the day's targets on French soil) when an unsuspecting Auster crossed his path. It provided Isken with his 50th kill. Awarded the Knight's Cross a fortnight after *Bodenplatte*, Isken was subsequently promoted to Leutnant; surviving the war with 56 victories, of which 17 were four-engined.

Having gambled and lost in the west, the Führer's attention perforce turned to the Soviet front. Russian forces were getting perilously close to

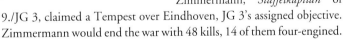

his capital, Berlin. In mid-January 1945 most of what remained of the *Jagdwaffe* was transferred eastwards. The final confrontation over the Western front on 14 January had cost a staggering 92 fighters, with a further 89 being lost in Defence of the Reich operations that day.

In the closing weeks of the war Homeland defence would rest squarely on the shoulders of the Focke-Wulf *Gruppen* and the new Me 262 jets. The few surviving Bf 109s subordinated to *Luftflotte Reich* (mainly those of JG 27) still scored the occasional individual success, but were powerless to avert the looming defeat.

As capitulation neared, the sole fighter presence on the Western front was provided by the Bf 109s of JG 53. Here, too, the pilots continued to inflict damage on the enemy until almost the very end, Oberleutnant Karl Broo, *Staffelkapitän* of 8.(later 5.)/JG 53, claiming eight US fighters between January and April 1945. This took his total to 13.

But perhaps the last of the old-time *Experten* to score in the west was Broo's *Gruppenkommandeur*, Major Julius Meimberg of II./JG 53. Joining JG 2 as a Leutnant in 1939, 'Jule' Meimberg's war against the western Allies had lasted six long years. It ended in the early evening of 13 April 1945 when his 53rd, and final, kill – fittingly a Spitfire, the Bf 109's traditional enemy in the west – went down in flames over the Black Forest.

Despite severe damage aft of the cockpit, the pilot of this G-14 – 'White 13' of 13./JG 53 – also succeeded in getting down in more or less one piece somewhere near Saarlautern early in 1945. Another group of inquisitive GIs look over the wreckage. Note the IV. *Gruppe* wavy bar superimposed on JG 53's black Defence of the Reich band

Oddly, this G-14, pictured in the foreground together with a group of surrendered Fw 190s at Bad Aibling after the cessation of hostilities, does not wear an identifying black Reich's Defence band, but has instead retained JG 53's famous 'Ace-of-Spades' badge on its cowling

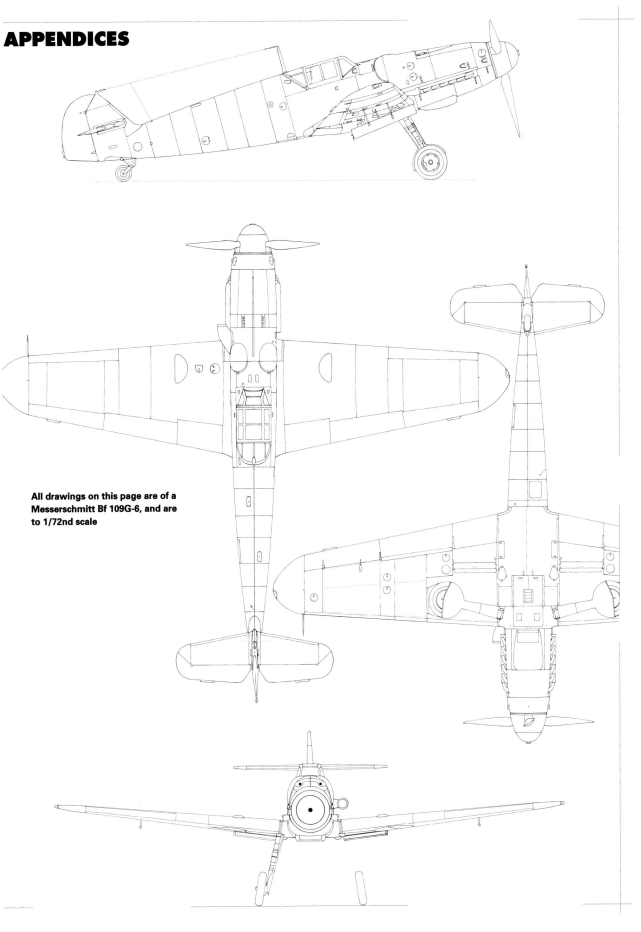

All drawings on this page are of a
Messerschmitt Bf 109G-6, and are
to 1/72nd scale

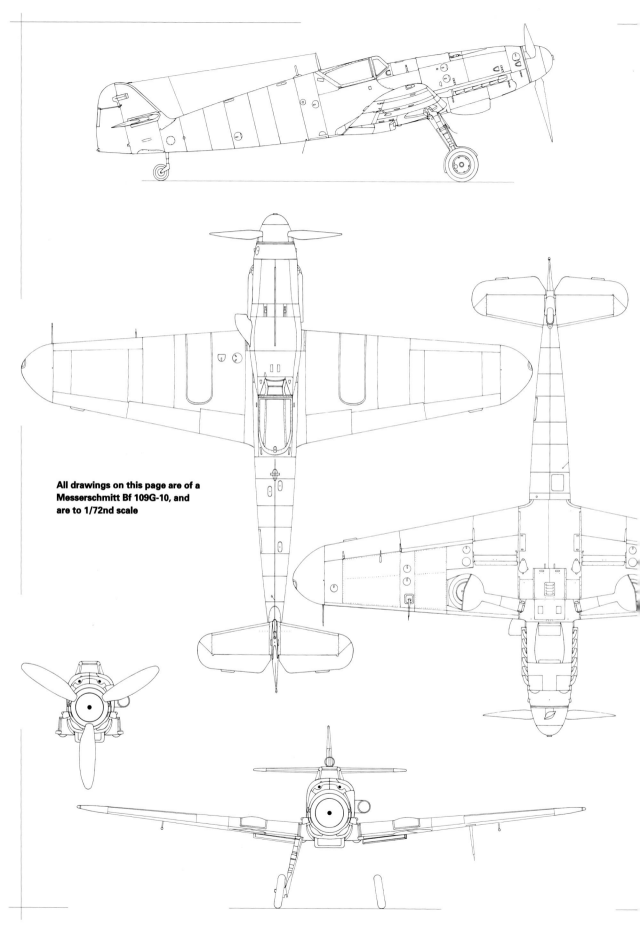

All drawings on this page are of a
Messerschmitt Bf 109G-10, and
are to 1/72nd scale

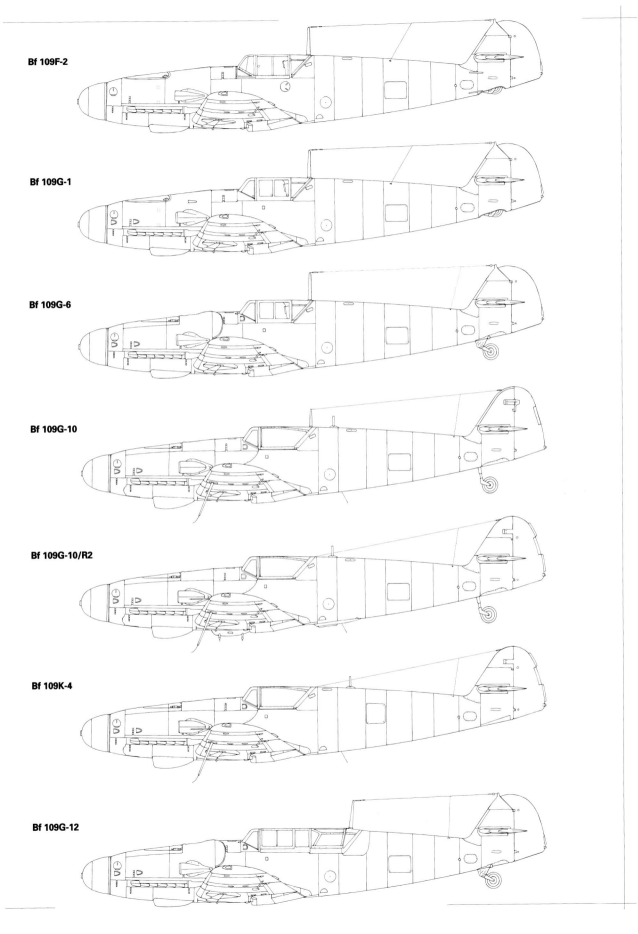

Bf 109F-2

Bf 109G-1

Bf 109G-6

Bf 109G-10

Bf 109G-10/R2

Bf 109K-4

Bf 109G-12

APPENDIX 1

Bf 109 Aces in the West with 50+ victories

	West	Total	JG(s)	Awards	
Galland, *GenLt* Adolf	104	104	27, 26	KOSD	
Mayer, *Obstlt* Egon	102	102	2	KOS	+
Priller, *Oberst* Josef	101	101	51, 26	KOS	
Lemke, *Hpt* Siegfried	95	96	2	K	
Wurmheller, *Hpt* Josef	93	102	53, 2	KOS	+
Schnell, *Hpt* Siegfried	87	93	2, 54	KO	+
Hackl, *Maj* Anton	73	192	77, 11, 76, 26, 300	KOS	
Bühligen, *Obstlt* Kurt	72	112	2	KOS	
Glunz, *Oblt* Adolf	71	71	52, 26, 7	KO	
Oesau, *Oberst* Walter	71	123	51, 3, 2, 1	KOS	+
Hahn, *Maj* Hans	68	108	54, 2	KO	
Mölders, *Oberst* Werner	68	115	53, 51	KOSD	+
Rollwage, *Lt* Herbert	60	71	53	KO	
Bär, *Obstlt* Heinz	59	220	51, 1, 3, EJG 2	KOS	
Ihlefeld, *Oberst* Herbert	56	130	77, 25, 11, 1	KOS	
Pflanz, *Oblt* Rudolf	52	52	2	K	+

Bf 109 Aces versus four-engined day bombers

	4-Eng	Total	JGs	Awards	
Schroer, *Maj* Werner	26	114	27, 54, 3	KOS	
Staiger, *Maj* Hermann	26	63	51, 26,1, 7	K	
Frey, *Hpt* Hugo	26	32	1, 11	K	+
Mayer, *Obstlt* Egon	25	102	2	KOS	+
Börngen, *Oblt* Ernst	24	45	27	K	
Bühligen, *Obstlt* Kurt	24	112	2	KOS	
Wurzer, *Hpt* Heinrich	23	26	302	-	
Müller, *Obstlt* Friedrich-Karl	22	140	53, 3	KO	+
Weik, *Oblt* Hans	22	36	3	K	

Key

KOSD = Knight's Cross, Oak leaves, Swords, Diamonds
+ = Killed during war

Note: Due to re-equipment, redesignations, transfers etc., it is not possible to say how many of the victories in the above lists were scored on the Fw 190. See text for further details

APPENDIX 2

Bf 109 Units in the West & Reich 1941-45

A: WEST August 1941

			Est/Serv
Jafü 3 (HQ: St Pol)			
Stab JG 2	Bf 109F-4	Beaumont-le-Roger	6 - 6
I./JG 2	Bf 109F-2	Brest/Morlaix	29 - 23
II./JG 2	Bf 109F-2	Abbeville-Drucat	30 - 20
III./JG 2	Bf 109F-2	St Pol-Bryas	39 - 23
Stab JG 26	Bf 109F-2	Audenbert	6 - 5
I./JG 26	Bf 109E-7	St Omer-Clairmarais	34 - 23
III./JG 26*	Bf 109F-2	Ligescourt	24 - 11

*minus 7. *Staffel* in North Africa

		Totals:	**168 - 111**

May 1944 (pre-D-Day)

II. Jagdkorps (HQ: Chantilly)
Jafü 4 (HQ: St Pol-Bryas)

III./JG 26	Bf 109G-6	Nancy	58 - 36

Jafü 5 (HQ: Bernay)

II./JG 2	Bf 109G-6	Creil	51 - 23

		Totals:	**109 - 59**

June 1944 (post-D-Day)

Jafü 4 (HQ: St Pol-Bryas)			
III./JG 26	Bf 109G-6	Villacoublay-Nord	31 - 16
I./JG 5	Bf 109G-6	Mons-en-Chaussée	14 - 9
II./JG 11	Bf 109G-6	Mons-en-Chaussée	19 - 5
I./JG 301	Bf 109G-6	Epinoy	13 - 13
Stab JG 27	Bf 109G-6	Champfleury	6 - 3
I./JG 27	Bf 109G-6	Vertus	39 - 24
III./JG 27	Bf 109G-6	Connantre	32 - 22
IV./JG 27	Bf 109G-6	Champfleury	31 - 19
Jafü 5 (HQ: Bernay)			
II./JG 2	Bf 109G-6	Creil	46 - 17
II./JG 3	Bf 109G-6	Guyancourt	(re-equipping)
III./JG 3	Bf 109G-6	Mareilly	23 - 15
II./JG 5	Bf 109G-6	Evreux	51 - 18
Jafü Bretagne (HQ: Brest)			
II./JG 53	Bf 109G-6	Vannes	32 - 9

		Totals:	**337 - 170**

B: REICH

September 1942
Luftwaffenbefehlshaber Mitte

I./JG 1	Bf 109F	Jever	67 - 53
IV./JG 1	Bf 109E/Fw 190A	Arnhem-Deelen	67 - 24
		Totals:	**134 - 77**

September 1944
Luftflotte Reich

Stab JG 3	Bf 109G	Königsberg (Neumark)	12 - 5
I./JG 3	Bf 109G	Borkheide	18 - 14
III./JG 4	Bf 109G	Alteno	68 - 58
II./JG 5	Bf 109G	Reinsdorf	24 - 9
III./JG 300	Bf 109G	Jüterborg	20 - 18
Stab JG 11	Bf 109G	Finsterwalde	- -
II./JG 27	Bf 109G	Finsterwalde	45 - 23
III./JG 53	Bf 109G	Mörtitz	52 - 36
I./JG 76	Bf 109G	Gahro	62 - 50
I./JG 302	Bf 109G	Schafstädt	25 - 13
Stab JG 300	Bf 109G	Erfurt-Bindersleben	5 - 3
I./JG 300	Bf 109G	Esperstedt	30 - 23
		Totals:	**361 - 252**

(Re-equipping post-Normandy)

III./JG 1	Bf 109G	Westerwald
II./JG 3	Bf 109G	Ziegenhain
I./JG 5	Bf 109G	Wunstorf
I./JG 27	Bf 109G	Rotenburg
IV./JG 27	Bf 109G	Hustedt
I./JG 301	Bf 109G	Salzwedel

Colour Plates

1

Bf 109F-4 (Wk-Nr 7059) 'White Double Chevron' of Major Dr Erich Mix, *Gruppenkommandeur* I./JG 1, Bergen aan Zee, Summer 1941

World War 1 veteran Dr Erich Mix had already served as *Gruppen-TO* (Technical Officer) of I./JG 53 and *Gruppenkommandeur* of III./JG 2 during the opening months of Word War 2 before assuming command of the embryonic I./JG 1 in the summer of 1941 – although, strictly speaking, he was not officially appointed *Kommandeur* until the *Gruppe* reached full establishment in September 1941. References are at odds as to his score in both wars, one of the more recent sources crediting him with two in World War 1 and three in World War 2. If this is the case, then the four bars marked here on the rudder of his *Friedrich* presumably include the two from the earlier conflict. In August 1942 Oberstleutnant Dr Erich Mix became *Geschwaderkommodore* of JG 1, before assuming staff duties as *Jafü Bretagne* (Fighter Leader Brittany) the following April.

2

Bf 109G-6 'White Double Chevron' of Hauptmann Friedrich Eberle, *Gruppenkommandeur* III./JG 1, Leeuwarden, October 1943

Far less pristine is this later *Kommandeur's* machine, which shows signs of much wear and tear, together with a considerable amount of overpainting. The chevrons, overlarge in comparison to those featured on the previous aircraft, are also slightly off the horizontal axis, giving them a distinctly asymmetrical appearance. Other marking points of interest are the white tail surfaces of a formation leader, absence of a vertical III. *Gruppe* bar behind the fuselage cross, and closely spiralled spinner – the two latter points were typical of III./JG 1 at this period (1942-43). Note also the *Erla* cockpit canopy (in unusual conjunction with a tall aerial mast) and underwing cannon gondola. In April 1944, with 18 kills to his credit, Eberle left III./JG 1 for other duties. Assuming command of the newly activated III./JG 4 three months later, he survived the war with 33 kills (24 in the west, including one 'heavy').

3

Bf 109F-4 (Wk-Nr 7558) 'Black Chevron and Bars' of Major Walter Oesau, *Geschwaderkommodore* JG 2 'Richthofen', St Pol, Autumn 1941

Oesau had been credited with 125 kills (including eight with the *Condor Legion*) before his death in action on 11 May 1944. This is one of two Bf 109Fs kept at readiness for him during his time as *Kommodore* of JG 2. The markings of both, although differing slightly, were based on the prewar pattern carried by biplane fighters – as were those of his entire *Stabsschwarm*.

4

Bf 109F-4 'Black Chevron and Crossed Bar(s)' of Oberleutnant Erich Leie *Geschwader-Adjutant* JG 2 'Richthofen', St Pol, Autumn 1941

As second-in-command to the *Geschwaderkommodore*, a pre-war adjutant's markings had then consisted of the same horizontal bars on either side of the fuselage cross, but minus the chevron. Erich Leie's machine sports these bars, but to them he has added a regulation set of wartime *Geschwader-Adjutant* symbols (a chevron and vertical bar) to produce the unique combination depicted here. Like the majority of those serving with the *Stabsschwarm* at this time, Leie subsequently converted to the Fw 190, but reverted to Bf 109s upon assuming command of JG 77 at the end of 1944. He was killed in a mid-air collision with a Soviet Yak-9 on 7 March 1945, his final score standing at 118 (43 in the west, including one 'heavy').

5

Bf 109F-4 'Black Bars and Dot' of Oberleutnant Rudolf Pflanz, *Geschwader-TO*, JG 2 'Richthofen', St Pol, Autumn 1941

The third member of a prewar biplane *Stabskette* also displayed two bars either side of the fuselage cross, but with a small rectangular dot above the leading bar. As the third man in Oesau's *Stabsschwarm*, Pflanz opted for the same, obviously deciding not to complicate matters further and eschewing a Technical Officer's wartime symbols of chevron, vertical bar and circle – although he did elect to keep a scoreboard on his rudder. One of the most successful Channel front pilots of this period, 'Rudi' Pflanz was appointed *Staffelkapitän* of 1./JG 2 in May 1942. He had amassed 52 victories (all in the west, including six on 23 July 1941) by the time he was killed in a dogfight with Spitfires near Abbeville on 31 July 1942.

6

Bf 109F-2 (Wk-Nr 5749) 'White Double Chevron' of Hauptmann Hans Hahn, *Gruppenkommandeur* III./JG 2 'Richthofen', St Pol, Summer 1941

A textbook set of command markings for the ebullient Hans 'Assi' Hahn, *Kommandeur* of III./JG 2, plus the 'rooster's head' *Gruppe* badge, which was a wordplay on his own name (Hahn meaning 'cockerel' in German). Note, too, the *Geschwader* emblem (soon to disappear from operational aircraft) below the windscreen, and the *Gruppenstab's* use of a narrow 'wraparound' band in place of a more usual III. *Gruppe* vertical bar on the aft fuselage. A further 37 western victories (including four 'heavies') would be added to the 31 depicted here by the time 'Assi' Hahn departed for the Eastern front, and command of II./JG 54. Forty Soviet victims took his final tally to 108 before engine damage forced him down behind enemy lines.

7

Bf 109F-4 (Wk-Nr 7650) 'Yellow 9' of Oberleutnant Erich Rudorffer, *Staffelkapitän* 6./JG 2 'Richthofen', Abbeville, Winter 1941-42

Rudorffer's *Friedrich* provides an example of the less common 71/02 upper surface camouflage colours of this period. Note also the discrepancy between the engine cowling and the finish of the rest of the fuselage. Such differences were the result of either using a replacement part, or removing the cowling for the sake of convenience when repainting/recamouflaging became necessary. Erich Rudorffer would score 74 kills as a member of JG 2, including 27 during II. *Gruppe's* deployment to Tunisia on the Fw 190. Like 'Assi' Hahn, he too subsequently commanded II./JG 54 on the Eastern front, where he added another 136 victories. He ended the war as *Kommandeur* of II./JG 7, claiming 12 kills on the Me 262 to take his final tally to an amazing 222!

8

Bf 109F-2 (Wk-Nr 6720) 'White 1' of Oberleutnant Egon Mayer, *Staffelkapitän* 7./JG 2 'Richthofen', St Pol, Summer 1941

Unlike Erich Rudorffer, Egon Mayer would remain with JG 2 throughout his entire operational career, from joining in December 1939 until his death in action (as *Kommodore*) in March 1944. Although a slow starter (it took Mayer 20 months to achieve the first 20 of the 23 kills depicted here), he became the first pilot to score 100 victories on the Western front. His final total of 102 included 25 four-engined bombers, but the majority of these successes were claimed after conversion to the Fw 190. As well as displaying its pilot's current score, this early *Friedrich* also proclaims Mayer's position as *Staffelkapitän* by the metal pennant (bearing the *Staffel* emblem) 'flying' from the aerial mast.

9

Bf 109F-4/B (Wk-Nr 7629) 'Blue 1 Chevron and Bar' of Oberleutnant Frank Liesendahl, *Staffelkapitän* 10.(*Jabo*)/JG 2 'Richthofen', Beamont-le-Roger, April 1942

An *Experte* of a different kind was Frank Liesendahl, *Kapitän* of JG 2's highly successful fighter-bomber *Staffel*. Liesendahl's own score has been meticulously recorded on the aircraft's rudder – the silhouettes of six freighters, totalling 27,500 BRT, sunk or damaged in the Channel between May 1941 and March 1942. This rudder was transferred from an earlier 'Blue 1' (F-2 Wk-Nr 12672) when the *Staffel* re-equipped. Note 10.(*Jabo*)/JG 2's tactical marking – a blue chevron and horizontal bar. The *Friedrichs* of neighbouring 10.(*Jabo*)/JG 26 displayed a white bomb in this position. Hauptmann Liesendahl was shot down while attacking a freighter off Brixham on 17 July 1942. He was awarded a posthumous Knight's Cross.

10

Bf 109G-1 (Wk-Nr 14063) 'White 11' of Oberleutnant Julius Meimberg, *Staffelkapitän* 11./JG 2 'Richthofen', Poix, Summer 1942

In mid-May 1942 1./JG 2 was sub-divided to form a new, specialised high-altitude *Staffel* (11./JG 2), equipped with pressurised Bf 109G-1s. Here, the external distinguishing features of this model can just be made out – the small inlet scoop for the air compressor above the supercharger intake, and the silica gel pellets inserted between the double-glazed cockpit panels to prevent condensation. Not visible is the vertical head armour behind the pilot, which acted as the cockpit's rear pressure bulkhead). 'Jule' Meimberg claimed 23 kills with JG 2 before leading his *Staffel* to North Africa, where it was assimilated into II./JG 53. He rose to command this *Gruppe* for the last year of the war, adding 30 more kills to his score – his 53rd, and final, victim was a Spitfire downed on 13 April 1945.

11

Bf 109F-2 (Wk-Nr 8117) 'White Triple Chevron' of Major Günther Lützow, *Geschwaderkommodore* JG 3, Auchy-au-Bois, May 1941

This otherwise standard F-2 displays the unusual, but not unique, 'triple chevron' *Kommodore* markings which 'Franzl' Lützow had first employed (albeit in black) on an earlier *Emil* towards the close of the Battle of Britain. In August 1942, after two years at the head of JG 3 – during which time his score had risen from 11 to 103 (all but eight achieved in the east) – Lützow embarked upon a series of staff appointments. He returned to combat in the closing stages of the war, joining the 'disgraced' Galland's Me 262-equipped JV 44. Oberst Günther Lützow was reported missing in action on 24 April 1945.

12

Bf 109G-10/AS 'Black Double Chevron' of Oberleutnant Alfred Seidl, *Gruppenkommandeur* I./JG 3 'Udet', Paderborn, December 1944

A late model *Gustav* – typified by clean cowling lines, *Erla* canopy, tall tail and lengthened tailwheel leg – bearing a wealth of markings. From front to rear: spiral spinner, *Geschwader* badge, *Kommandeur's* chevrons, fuselage *Balkenkreuz* and JG 3's white Defence of the Reich band. The small '8' below the cockpit is Seidl's personal marking, a momento of his earlier service with III./JG 53, where he always flew aircraft No '8'. Unusually, the machine does not carry underwing crosses. Seidl did not add to the 31 kills he had scored with JG 53 during his three months as *Kommandeur* of I./JG 3, nor during the final weeks of the war flying the Me 262 with JG 7.

13

Bf 109G-6 (Wk-Nr 26058) 'Double Chevron' of Major Kurt Brändle, *Gruppenkommandeur* II./JG 3 'Udet', Schiphol, October 1943

More obviously a *Gustav*, with the distinctive cowling '*Beulen*' (bulges) which covered the spent casing chutes of the G-6's heavier MG 131 fuselage machine guns, this machine wears a dense dapple camouflage. In addition to the white rudder of a formation leader, points of interest include the *Geschwader's* 'Winged U' badge, which is shown reversed (as carried by many II./JG 3 aircraft of this period), and the outline-only command chevrons and II. *Gruppe* horizontal bar. Although sometimes seen on earlier *hellblau*-sided *Emils*, this style of marking was not common later in the war. Another ex-member of JG 53, all but 25 of Brändle's final tally of 180 kills had been scored in the east. He lost his life in this aircraft on 3 November 1943.

14

Bf 109G-6 'Double Chevron 1' of Hauptmann Walther Dahl, *Gruppenkommandeur* III./JG 3 'Udet', Bad Wörishofen, September 1943

Another white-ruddered *Kommandeur's* machine, this time with the *Geschwader* badge pointing in the right direction! Note, however, that whereas the command chevrons are edged in white, the III. *Gruppe* vertical bar aft of the fuselage cross is plain black, as was customary for all III./JG 3 aircraft at this time. Although better known as an Fw 190 *Sturm Experte* (see *Osprey Aircraft of the Aces 9*), over half of Walther Dahl's final total of 128 kills were scored on the Bf 109, including at least 17 of the 36 heavy bombers he claimed. After serving as *Kommodore* of JG 300, Oberst Dahl was appointed *Inspekteur der Tagjäger* (Inspector of Day Fighters) on 26 January 1945.

15

Bf 109G-6/AS (Wk-Nr 412179) 'Black 14' of Unteroffizier Horst Petzschler, 2./JG 3 'Udet', Burg bei Madgeburg, May 1944

Included to illustrate the overall light blue-grey (RLM 76) scheme briefly adopted by several high-altitude units, the 'low-visibility' finish and markings of 'Black 14' are more than somewhat compromised by the black-and-white spiral spinner – III./JG 1 would go even further, adding Defence of the Reich red bands(!) to their otherwise *hellgrau* Bf 109G-14/AS fighters. Petzschler claimed four US aircraft – two fighters and two heavy bombers – while with 2./JG 3. Although Wk-Nr 412179 was lost in a dogfight east of Madgeburg on 30 May 1944 (killing pilot Feldwebel Otto Büssow), Petzschler returned to his previous unit, JG 51, and survived the war with 27 victories.

16

Bf 109G-6y 'White 1' of Hauptmann Karl-Heinz Langer, *Staffelkapitän* 7./JG 3 'Udet', Bad Wörishofen, Autumn 1943

Another 'specialised' G-6 sub-variant was the 'y', fitted with FuG 16ZY radio (note additional underfuselage antenna level with cockpit), which was issued primarily to formation leaders to permit airborne control by radio. Of much more visual interest, however, is 7. *Staffel's* spectacular 'shooting star' marking, said to have been inspired by the underwing rockets with which they had earlier been equipped (9./JG 3 carried an equally distinctive marking – a black-and-white 'eye', painted on the yellow *Beulen* of their G-6s). Major Karl-Heinz Langer ended the war as *Kommandeur* of III./JG 3, and with at least 30 victories, the last few of which were claimed in the closing weeks amid the chaos and confusion of the Eastern front.

17

Bf 109G-14/ASy 'Black 13' of Oberleutnant Ernst Scheufele, *Staffelkapitän* 14./JG 4, Reinersdorf, October 1944

Combining a high-altitude DB 605AS engine (and its associated 'unbulged' cowl) with FuG 16ZY radio equipment, Scheufele's 'Black 13' also offers another example of Defence of the Reich aft fuselage markings. At least 18 units involved in Reich's Defence operations were assigned such an identifying band, or bands, in varying colours, but not all reportedly applied them to their aircraft. Note, too, IV./JG 4's abbreviated 'wavy bar' *Gruppe* symbol superimposed on the bands, and the personal inscription *Peterle* below the cockpit. Previously a member of JG 5, Ernst Scheufele was brought down by ground fire near Aachen on 3 December 1944. His final total of 18 victories including three 'heavies'.

18

Bf 109G-5/AS (Wk-Nr 110064) 'Grey Double Chevron' of Major Günther Specht, Gruppenkommandeur II./JG 11, Wunstorf, April 1944

The indomitable Günther Specht, who lost an eye in an attack on a RAF bomber over the German Bight in December 1939, nevertheless returned to combat flying, first with ZG 26 and later with JG 11. Pictured at the time of his winning the Knight's Cross (on 8 April 1944 with 31 victories), his AS-engined Gustav displays signs of considerable overspraying. It also carries JG 1's seldom-seen Geschwader badge. This latter, based upon 'The Guardian' by Arno Breker (Hitler's favourite sculptor) had only recently supplanted Specht's personal 'winged pencil' badge, which had graced all his previous aircraft (see Osprey Aircraft of the Aces 25). After a year at the head of II. Gruppe, Specht was appointed Geschwaderkommodore of JG 11 in May 1944. He was killed near Maastricht during Operation Bodenplatte, his final score of 34 including 15 four-engined bombers.

19

Bf 109G-6 'Black Double Chevron' of Hauptmann Anton Hackl, Gruppenkommandeur III./JG 11, Oldenburg, January 1944

Although devoid of any unit markings (save the Geschwader's yellow Defence of the Reich band), Hackl's G-6 'Kanonenboot' carries a meticulous scoreboard on its formation leader's white rudder – a garlanded Knight's Cross with Oak Leaves and the figure 100, plus 33 further individual kill bars. At this juncture of his career Hackl had two aircraft at his disposal: an Fw 190A-6 for his anti-bomber activities (see Osprey Aircraft of the Aces 9 profile No 24) and the Gustav depicted here for fighter operations. 'Toni' Hackl relinquished leadership of III./JG 11 in May 1944. After several intervening commands (including those of JG 76, II./JG 26 and JG 300), he returned to JG 11 as Geschwaderkommodore in February 1945. He ended the war with 192 victories, his western successes, totalling 73, including 32 four-engined bombers – the majority, if not all, of the latter were brought down while flying the Fw 190.

20

Bf 109G-1 'Black 1' of Leutnant Heinz Knoke, Staffelkapitän 5./JG 11, Jever May 1943

Pictured towards the close of his 'high-altitude bombing career' (the seventh kill bar on the rudder represents a B-17 brought down near Husum on 14 May 1943 by a frontal pass after his 250-kg bomb had failed to detonate), Knoke's pressurised G-1 carries both the Gruppe badge – previously that of I./JG 1, but dating back even earlier to the unit's origins as the Jagdstaffel Holland – and his own personal insignia (intertwined wedding rings with the name of his wife, Lilo, above). Later to command III./JG 1, Knoke was seriously wounded in October 1944. His 44 victories, including 19 heavy bombers, were all gained in the west, and all flying the Bf 109.

21

Bf 109T (Wk-Nr 7767) 'Black 6' of Oberleutnant Herbert Christmann, Staffelkapitän 11./JG 11, Lister/Norway, Spring 1944

One of the last units to fly the little-known Bf 109T (designed to operate from, but destined never to serve aboard, the aircraft carrier Graf Zeppelin) was 11./JG 11, the ex-Jagdstaffel Helgoland. This gaudily decorated example was the mount of the Staffelkapitän. Although the ultimate fate of 'Black 6' is unknown (one source states that it was lost in the late spring of 1944 when Christmann was forced to take to his parachute, or alternatively it may have been one of the few surviving Tonis which 11./JG 11 passed on to IV./JG 5 in June 1944), it is on record that Christmann was appointed to the command of the Fw 190-equipped 1./JG 11 on the Normandy front, where he was killed on 20 August 1944. His exact score is also uncertain, but it numbered at least five, including a brace of B-17s.

22

Bf 109F-2 (Wk-Nr 6714) 'Black Chevron and Bars' of Oberstleutnant Adolf Galland, Geschwaderkommodore JG 26 'Schlageter', Brest-Guipavas, April 1941

One of the first Friedrichs flown by Galland, Wk-Nr 6714 wears standard Channel front finish for spring 1941 with all-yellow cowling and spinner, and matching rudder. The 60 kill bars are a record of his score to date, the first 58 (in red) having been achieved on earlier Emils, and the last two (in black) believed to indicate successes gained on the Bf 109F. The telescope protruding through the windscreen (mounted to the right of the standard gunsight) was used solely for purposes of long-range identification and was not, itself, a telescopic gunsight.

23

Bf 109F-2/U 'Black Chevron and Bars' of Oberstleutnant Adolf Galland, Geschwaderkommodore JG 26 'Schlageter', Audembert, November 1941

Like many Emil Experten, Galland soon came to regard the Friedrich as a retrograde step, with its single cannon firing through the propeller hub a poor substitute for the former's two wing cannon. In an effort to 'beef up' what he considered to be the undergunned Bf 109F, Galland had two 'specials' converted for his own use. The first, pictured here, had the two MG 17 machine guns above the engine replaced by heavier MG 131s (necessitating the small fairing shown, which was the forerunner of the Gustav's distinctive 'Beulen'), whilst the second was fitted with two wing cannon similar to the Bf 109E. Both carried near identical markings, with the yellow on the nose now restricted to the undercowling only, the Geschwader's Gothic 'S' badge giving way to Galland's personal 'Mickey Mouse' insignia, and a total of 94 victories recorded on the rudder. Galland would have a long wait for the coveted 100, Mölders' unexpected death 'sentencing' him to three years' service as Göring's General der Jagdflieger. The last seven of his 104 kills were scored on the Me 262 in the closing months of the war (see Osprey Aircraft of the Aces 17).

24

Bf 109F-2 'Black Double Chevron' of Hauptmann Gerhard Schöpfel, Gruppenkommandeur III./JG 26 'Schlageter', Liegescourt, Summer 1941

Gerhard Schöpfel succeeded Adolf Galland both as Kommandeur of III./JG 26 and, later, Geschwaderkommodore of JG 26. One of the aircraft he flew in the former role was this Friedrich, which bears very modestly proportioned command chevrons. Numbered among the most successful pilots at the height of the cross-Channel campaigning, all 40+ of Schöpfel's victories (references differ between 40 and 45) were claimed with JG 26. Between various staff postings he subsequently, and briefly, commanded both JG 4 (at the time of the Normandy invasion) and JG 6 during the final month of the war.

25

Bf 109G-6 'Black 22' of Major Klaus Mietusch, *Gruppenkommandeur* III./JG 26 'Schlageter', Lille-Nord, Spring 1944

One of Schöpfel's successors at the head of III./JG 26 was Klaus Mietusch, another long-serving member of the 'Schlageter' *Geschwader*, with whom he scored all 70+ (again sources vary) of his kills – including 15 on the Eastern front as *Staffelkapitän* of 7./JG 26, and 16 four-engined bombers in the west. This *Gustav* illustrates III. *Gruppe's* later practice of identifying their *Stab* aircraft with double figures commencing with '20', rather than command chevrons and symbols. Mietusch's incident-packed career finally ended with 'Black 25', the machine in which he was shot down by a P-51 on 17 September 1944.

26

Bf 109F-2 'Black 13' of Oberleutnant Gustav Sprick, *Staffelkapitän* 8./JG 26 'Schlageter', Liegescourt, June 1941

A third 'Schlageter' *Experte*, all of whose 31 kills – the last eight on the *Friedrich* – had been scored with the one unit (in Sprick's case the 8. 'Adamson' *Staffel*, so named after the cartoon character seen here below the cockpit, which provided the *Staffel's* emblem). Such insignia, *and* Gustav 'Micky' Sprick, would soon be no more, the former disappearing by official edict, and the latter becoming yet another victim of the early *Friedrich's* structural weakness when the starboard wing of his machine collapsed during a dogfight with Spitfires near St Omer on 28 June 1941.

27

Bf 109G-6 trop (Wk-Nr 140139) 'Black Double Chevron' of Major Ernst Düllberg, *Gruppenkommandeur* III./JG 27, Wiesbaden-Erbenheim, March 1944

Recently returned from the eastern Mediterranean (witness the white aft fuselage theatre band and dust filter fitted to the supercharger air intake), Düllberg's *Gustav* also wears the all-white vertical tail surfaces of a *Gruppenkommandeur*, with 27 kill markings carefully applied. Düllberg would add another nine, including five 'heavies', while leading the *Gruppe* in Defence of the Reich operations, and before departing to take command of JG 76 in September. His reported total by war's end was 50, ten of which were four-engined bombers.

28

Bf 109G-6 'Yellow 1' of Leutnant Dr Peter Werfft, *Staffelkapitän* 9./JG 27, Vienna-Seyring, March 1944

What a difference a few days can make. The overpainting of the white Mediterranean band with JG 27's 'official' Defence of the Reich sage-green has completely altered the appearance of this G-6 *'Kanonenboot'*. The 11 kills marked here on the formation leader's white tail (rudders only for JG 27's *Staffelkapitäne*) would be joined by 15 more – all but four of them heavy bombers – before the year was out. Dr Peter Werfft, one of the oldest operational pilots in the entire *Jagdwaffe*, ended the war as *Kommandeur* of III./JG 27. His last two kills – a pair of P-38s – were claimed on 27 December

1944 at the height of the Ardennes counter-offensive, and more than two months after his 40th birthday!

29

Bf 109G-6 (Wk-Nr 15913) 'Red 1' of Major Hermann Graf, *Gruppenkommandeur* JG(r) 50, Wiesbaden-Erbenheim, September 1943

Another *'Kanonenboot'*, this one the mount of Major Hermann Graf during his tenure of office as *Kommandeur* of the single *Gruppe*-strong JG 50 in the late summer/early autumn of 1943. The rudder meticulously records all of Graf's Eastern front victories, the number 172 (for which he received the Diamonds), surmounted and surrounded by his initials and the award ribbon, plus two rows of 15 individual bars each. The last three bars are for recent western successes, including two B-17s downed on 6 September. Later briefly commanding both JGs 1 and 11, Hermann Graf would claim a total of ten kills (at least half of them four-engined bombers) in Defence of the Reich operations before returning to the east and his old unit, JG 52. This aircraft is also featured on the cover artwork, although it is seen here at a later stage in its brief career devoid of the yellow under-cowling and chin intake, and with the 'Red 1' outlined in black rather than white.

30

Bf 109G-6 'White 10' of Oberleutnant Alfred Grislawski, *Staffelkapitän* of 1./JG 50, Wiesbaden-Erbenheim, September 1943

Apart from the addition of the *Staffel* badge below the cockpit (in place of the *Kommandeur's* elaboarte nose decoration), the G-6 flown by Alfred Grislawski (himself an ex-JG 52 Eastern front *Experte* who had accompanied Graf back to the Reich) displays markings very similar to those above, even down to the rudder scoreboard recording his successes to date– the number 40, which had won Grislawski the Knight's Cross, encircled by his initials and the award ribbon, plus another 72 individual bars. The last three again denote recent victories in the west with JG 50. Unlike Graf, however, Alfred Grislawski did not return to the Russian front, subsequently serving instead as a *Staffelkapitän* with both JGs 1 and 53. While so doing he won the Oak Leaves and added another 20 western kills to the four he had ultimately scored with JG 50. This brought his total to 133, 18 of which were 'heavies'.

31

Bf 109F-1 (Wk-Nr 5628) of Major Werner Mölders, *Geschwaderkommodore* JG 51, St Omer, November 1940

One of the first *Friedrich's* to reach the frontline, this aircraft was also Werner Mölders' first Bf 109F, and it was photographed still bearing traces of the original four-letter delivery *Stammkennzeichen* (SG+GW), but with no command markings yet applied (apparently the all-important rudder scoreboard took priority). The last of the 54 victories shown here represented a Hurricane claimed on 29 October 1940.

32

Bf 109F-1 'Black Double Chevron and Bars' of Major Werner Mölders, *Geschwaderkommodore* JG 51, Mardyck, April 1941

Another five months and nine victories later, a very different *Friedrich* indeed has emerged, complete with *Geschwader* badge and a full set of *Kommodore's* markings. This time the last victory bar on the rudder (No 63) denotes a Spitfire brought down on 15 April 1941. Five more would be added before JG 51 decamped for the Eastern front. There, Oberstleutnant Werner Mölders would claim another 33 kills before his elevation to *General der Jagdflieger*.

33

Bf 109F-2 (Wk-Nr 8155) 'Black Double Chevron' of Hauptmann Karl-Heinz Leesmann, *Gruppenkommandeur* I./JG 52, Leeuwarden, Summer 1941

Although JG 52 is indissolubly linked with the Eastern front, I. *Gruppe* did not participate in the opening weeks of Operation *Barbarossa*, its component *Staffeln* instead remaining dispersed about the German Bight until September 1941. Leesmann's machine displays both the *Gruppe* badge (a charging boar) behind the fuselage cross, and his personal score of 20 kills on the tailfin. Two more victories would earn him the Knight's Cross on 23 July 1941. Seriously wounded in Russia in November 1941, Leesmann did not return to combat flying until March 1943 when he assumed command of III./JG 1. During the next four months he claimed four more kills (including two B-17s) to bring his final score to 37, before he was himself shot down over the North Sea on 25 July 1943.

34

Bf 109F-2 (Wk-Nr 6683) 'Black Chevron and Bars' of Major Günther von Maltzahn, *Geschwaderkommodore* JG 53 '*Pik-As*', St Omer-Wizernes, May 1941

Bearing a striking resemblance to the previous profile (except for the different *Geschwader* badge and rudder scoreboard), this *Friedrich* is also pictured shortly before departure for the east. The 20 kill bars shown here are believed to include four 'balloon-bustings', for *Frhr* von Maltzahn's last victory in the west (a Spitfire downed on 9 May) was reputedly his 16th – to that would be added 33 in Russia and 19 in the Mediterranean. 'Henri' Maltzahn relinquished command of JG 53 in October 1943, serving out the remainder of the war in staff positions.

35

Bf 109F-2 (Wk-Nr 6674) 'Black Double Chevron' of Hauptmann Heinz Bretnütz, *Gruppenkommandeur* of II./JG 53 '*Pik-As*', St Omer-Clairmarais, May 1941

Points of interest here are the attempt to 'tone down' the yellow cowling and spinner with dark green mottling, the windscreen mounted telescope (like Galland's, to the right of the standard gunsight), the name *Peter* below the cockpit, and the impressive tally of kills on the rudder. 'Pietsch' Bretnütz's score of 32 was exactly double that of his *Kommodore* by the time the 'Ace-of-Spades' *Geschwader* departed the Channel front for the invasion of Russia. His 33rd, and last kill (a Tupolev SB-2 twin-engined bomber) was achieved in the opening minutes of *Barbarossa*, after which Bretnütz himself had to forceland. Five days later he died of the injuries he had sustained.

36

Bf 109F-2 'Black Double Chevron' of Hauptmann Wolf-Dietrich Wilcke, *Gruppenkommandeur* III./JG 53 '*Pik-As*', Berck-sur-Mer, May 1941

Another of von Maltzahn's *Kommandeure* immediately prior to *Barbarossa* was III. *Gruppe's* '*Fürst*' Wilcke, who was also des-

tined to become a leading figure in the ranks of the *Jagdwaffe*. Just visible below the windscreen is Wilcke's miniature monogram. The 13 kills shown here had all been scored on the *Emil*. And although it was in the east that Wilcke found true fame and success, he later returned to the Reich as *Kommodore* of JG 3, achieving the last six of his 162 victories early in 1944, before himself falling victim to P-51s on 23 March of that year.

37

Bf 109G-6 'Black 2' of Oberfeldwebel Herbert Rollwage, 5./JG 53 '*Pik-As*', Vienna-Seyring, January 1944

Rollwage was one of JG 53's most experienced NCO pilots, the white formation leader's rudder on his G-6 '*Kanonenboot*' presumably indicating his position as a *Schwarmführer*, while the rust-red fuselage band (a darker shade than JG 1's later 'official' Defence of the Reich colour) denotes II./JG 53's twinning with the '*Wilde Sau*' II./JG 301 at this juncture. The last two of the 49 victories shown here represent a brace of P-38s destroyed on 7 January 1944. All 70+ of Herbert Rollwage's kills, which included 14 'heavies', were scored with JG 53.

38

Bf 109K-4 'Yellow 1' of Leutnant Günther Landt, *Staffelkapitän* 11./JG 53 '*Pik-As*', Kirrlach, February 1945

'Micki' Landt's Bf 109K-4, wearing a typical late-war finish of dark brown and green over *hellgrau* 76, also displays JG 53's black Reich's Defence aft fuselage band. Note, however, that the *Geschwader's* famous 'Ace-of-Spades' badge, which had been sported continuously from the first day of hostilities (with the exception of the famous *contretemps* during the Battle of Britain – see *Osprey Aircraft of the Aces 11*), is no longer carried, the band alone now serving as a means of unit identification. Out of Landt's final total of 20+, at least 12 (all fighters) were scored in the final eight months of the war.

39

Bf 109G-6 (Wk-Nr 440141) 'Yellow 1' of Oberleutnant Wilhelm Schilling, *Staffelkapitän* 9./JG 54, Ludwigslust, February 1944

This 'Yellow 1', wearing the blue Defence of the Reich band assigned to III./JG 54, also displays a full set of unit badges – the *Geschwader's* 'Green Heart' below the cockpit, with III. *Gruppe's* shield superimposed, plus 9. *Staffel's* 'Grinning Devil' on the engine cowling. Although Wk-Nr 440141 was downed on 20 February 1944, Wilhelm Schilling survived his wounds – and the war – reportedly with a final total of 50 kills.

40

Bf 109K-4 (Wk-Nr 330204) 'White 1' of Hauptmann Menzel, *Staffelkapitän* 9./JG 77, Neuruppin, December 1944

Included primarily to illustrate JG 77's white-green Reich's Defence fuselage bands, 'White 1' also displays a tell-tale diamond-shaped patch on the engine cowling where the *Geschwader's* 'Ace-of-Hearts' badge has been overpainted (coincident with the application of the bands). This machine was not flown solely by the *Staffelkapitän*, and was being piloted by Leutnant Herbert Abendroth when it crash-landed during *Bodenplatte*. Although Abendroth was credited with three kills prior to his capture on 1 January 1945, records detailing Hauptmann Menzel's final score appear to have been lost after the war.

Bibliography

(Bibliography continued from title verso page)

CONSTABLE, TREVOR J and TOLIVER, COL RAYMOND F, *Horrido! Fighter Aces of the Luftwaffe.* Macmillan, New York, 1968

DIERICH, WOLFGANG, *Die Verbände der Luftwaffe 1935-1945.* Motorbuch Verlag, Stuttgart, 1976

ENGAU, FRITZ, *Frontal durch die Bomberpulks.* Hoppe Verlag, Graz, 1997

FREEMAN, ROGER A, *Mighty Eighth War Diary.* Jane's, London, 1981

GALLAND, ADOLF, *The First and the Last.* Methuen, London, 1953

GIRBIG, WERNER, *. . . im Anflug auf die Reichshauptstadt.* Motorbuch Verlag, Stuttgart, 1970

GIRBIG, WERNER, *Start im Morgengrauen.* Motorbuch Verlag, Stuttgart, 1973

GIRBIG, WERNER, *Jagdgeschwader 5 'Eismeerjäger'.* Motorbuch Verlag, Stuttgart, 1976

GREEN, WILLIAM, *Augsburg Eagle: The Story of the Messerschmitt 109.* Macdonald, London, 1971

HAGEN, HANS PETER, *Husaren des Himmels.* Erich Pabel Verlag, Rastatt, 1964

HAMMEL, ERIC, *Air War Europa: America's Air War against Germany: Chronology 1942-1945.* Pacifica Press, California, 1994

HELD, WERNER, *Die Deutsche Tagjagd.* Motorbuch Verlag, Stuttgart, 1977

HELD, WERNER; *Reichsverteidigung: Die Deutsche Tagjagd 1943-1945.* Podzun-Pallas, Friedberg, 1988

ISHOVEN, ARMAND VAN, *Messerschmitt Bf 109 at War.* Ian Allan, Shepperton, 1977

KNOKE, HEINZ, *I Flew for the Führer.* Evans, London, 1953

LOTZE, K H, *. . . und es saust der Frack.* Kurt Vowinckel Verlag, Neckargemünd, 1961

MARSHALL, FRANCIS L, *Sea Eagles: The Messerschmitt Bf 109T.* Air Research, Walton on Thames, 1993

MEHNERT, KURT AND TEUBER, REINHARD, *Die deutsche Luftwaffe 1939-1945.* Militär-Verlag Patzwall, Norderstedt, 1996

MOMBEEK, ERIC, *Defending the Reich: The History of Jagdgeschwader 1 'Oesau'.* JAC Publications, Norwich, 1992

MOMBEEK, ERIC, *Luftwaffe: A Pictorial History.* Crowood, Marlborough, 1997

MOMBEEK, ERIC, *Sturmjäger: Zur Geschichte des Jagdgeschwaders 4.* Linkebeek, 1997

NAUROTH, HOLGER, *Jagdgeschwader 2 'Richthofen': Eine Bildchronik.* Motorbuch Verlag, Stuttgart, 1999

OBERMEIER, ERNST, *Die Ritterkreuzträger der Luftwaffe 1939-1945: Band I, Jagdflieger.* Verlag Dieter Hoffmann, Mainz, 1966

OFFICIAL, *The Rise and Fall of The German Air Force (1933 to 1945).* Air Ministry, London, 1948

PARKER, DANNY S, *To Win the Winter Sky: Air War over the Ardennes 1944-1945.* Greenhill Books, London, 1994

PIEKALKIEWICZ, JANUSZ, *Luftkrieg 1939-1945.* Südwest Verlag, Munich, 1978

PRIEN, JOCHEN, *Geschichte des Jagdgeschwaders 53 (3 vols).* Flugzeug 1989 (vol 1)/Struwe Druck, Eutin, 1990

PRIEN, JOCHEN, *Geschichte des Jagdgeschwaders 77 (4 vols).* Struwe Druck, 1992-

PRIEN, JOCHEN/RODEIKE, PETER, *Jagdgeschwader 1 and 11 (3 vols).* Struwe Druck, Eutin

PRIEN, JOCHEN/RODEIKE, PETER, *Messerschmitt Bf 109F, G & K Series.* Schiffer, Atglen, 1993

PRIEN, JOCHEN/RODEIKE, PETER/STEMMER, GERHARD; *Jagdgeschwader 27 (4 vols of individual Gruppe histories).* Struwe Druck, Eutin

PRIEN, JOCHEN/STEMMER, GERHARD; *Jagdgeschwader 3 (4 vols of individual Gruppe histories).* Struwe Druck, Eutin

PRICE, Dr ALFRED, *The Last Year of the Luftwaffe: May 1944 to May 1945.* Arms & Armour, London, 1991

PRICE, Dr ALFRED, *The Luftwaffe Data Book.* Greenhill Books, London 1997

PRILLER, JOSEF, *Geschichte eines Jagdgeschwaders: Das JG 26 (Schlageter) von 1937 bis 1945.* Kurt Vowinckel Verlag, Neckargemünd, 1965

RESCHKE, WILLI; *Jagdgeschwader 301/302 'Wilde Sau'.* Motorbuch Verlag, Stuttgart, 1998

RIES jr, KARL, *Dora Kurfürst und rote 13 (vols I-IV).* Verlag Dieter Hoffmann, Finthen/Mainz, 1964-69

RIES jr, KARL, *Markings and Camouflage Systems of Luftwaffe Aircraft in World War II (vols I-IV).* Verlag Dieter Hoffmann, Finthen/Mainz, 1963-62

RIES jr, KARL/OBERMAIER, ERNST, *Bilanz am Seitenleitwerk.* Verlag Dieter Hoffmann, Finthen/Mainz, 1970

RING, HANS/GIRBIG, WERNER, *Jagdgeschwader 27.* Motorbuch verlag, Stuttgart, 1971

SCHRAMM, PERCY ERNST (ed), *Die Niederlage 1945.* DTV, Munich, 1962

SCHRAMM, PERCY E. (ed), *Kriegstagebuch des OKW (8 vols).* Manfred Pawlak, Herrsching, 1982

SCHREIER, HANS, *JG 52: Das erfolgreichste Jagdgeschwader des II. Weltkrieges.* Kurt Vowinckel Verlag, Berg am See, 1990

SHORES, CHRISTOPHER, *Air Aces.* Bison Books, Greenwich, 1983

STIPDONK, PAUL/MEYER, MICHAEL, *Das JG 51: Eine Bilddokumentation über die Jahre 1938-1945.* Heinz Nickel, Zweibrücken, 1996

MAGAZINES AND PERIODICALS (VARIOUS ISSUES)
Adler, Der
Aeroplane, The
Berliner Illustrierte Zeitung
Flieger Revue
Flight
Flug-Revue International
Flugzeug
Flugzeug Archiv
Jägerblatt
Jet & Prop
Jet & Prop Archiv
Militärhistorische Schriftenreihe
Signal
Truppendienst
Wehrwissenschaftliche Rundschau